Hiroshi Tasaka Talks about the Future of Humanity

The *Twelve Insights* to Foresee the Future

This English edition is published in 2024 by Babel Press, 6013 N Palm Ave. Fresno, CA 93704, U.S.A. under permission of and by arrangement with the author.

This book was originally published in Japanese under the title

"田坂広志　人類の未来を語る"

by Kobunsha Co., Ltd., Tokyo, Japan in 2023.

Cover design:　Yuko Yoshida
DTP:　Yoko Imatabilawchuk
Translation:　Babel Transmedia Center

4

Table of Contents

Amazing and Visionary Book

Jacques Attali

I strongly recommend this amazing and visionary book.

As a new step in the global work of the author,

he insists on the new ideology based on Rational Altruism,

as the basis of a new global economic and social model.

A must read for anyone

who want to understand the future and be prepared for it.

Jacques Attali
Economist, Thinker, Author
Advisor to the President of France, François Mitterrand
The First President of
the European Bank for Reconstruction and Development

opale.photo/ALFO

The Origin of This Book and How to Read It

An E-mail from Dr. Jacques Attali

Hiroshi Tasaka Talks about the Future of Humanity

The catalyst for this book was
a single e-mail.

On April 9, 2021,
I received an e-mail from Dr. Jacques Attali,
who is known as one of **Europe's most brilliant intellectuals**.
He served as an advisor to French President Mitterrand
and was the first President of
the European Bank for Reconstruction and Development.

It was an honor for me to receive Dr. Attali's message.
In it, he told me how profoundly impressed he was
after reading my book *The Five Laws to Foresee the Future*
in English, and expressed a desire to hear more about it.

This book is the English version of my Japanese book,
Mirai o yoken suru "itsutsu no hōsoku".
It interprets the future of humanity using the idea of
dialectic
as developed by Georg Wilhelm Friedrich Hegel,
an 18th-century German idealist philosopher
considered one of the greatest thinkers in human history.

The *Five Laws* of **Hegel's dialectic**
presented in this book are as follows:

The First Law:
   *The Law of Development through **Spiral Process***
The Second Law:
   *The Law of Development through **Negation of Negation***
The Third Law:
   *The Law of Development through **Transformation from***
   Quantity to Quality
The Fourth Law:
   *The Law of Development through **Interpenetration of***
   Opposing Objects
The Fifth Law:
   *The Law of Development through **Sublation of***
Contradiction

By using these laws, it is remarkable
how well we can foresee the future of various things.
This is why I have employed these **Five Laws**
to foresee the future in my various publications.

Dr. Attali was deeply impressed and intrigued by
my method of
foreseeing the future through dialectical thinking.
This led him to send me the e-mail mentioned above.
In response to Dr. Attali's request,
I conducted a ***series of lectures***
in which I chose a topic each month and
discussed the future of that topic.

These lectures were conducted via e-mail in English
from May 2021 to April 2022.

The themes I covered were:

1. *Hegelian Dialectic*
2. *The Imagination of Science Fiction (SF)*
3. *Complex Systems in Society*
4. *The Era of Pandemics*
5. *The Revolution of Artificial Intelligence (AI)*
6. *Genetic Engineering*
7. *The Future of the Economy*
8. *The Future of Capitalism*
9. *The Future of Democracy*
10. *The Future of Religion*
11. *The Future of Art*
12. *The Possibility of Immortality*

Each of these **twelve themes** is an important topic
concerning the **future of humanity**, and in my lectures,
I candidly shared my insights and foresights.

Upon completing these twelve themes,
I decided to compile into a book
the **twelve insights about the future of humanity**
discussed in these lectures.
Additionally, I revised and made additions to
The Five Laws to Foresee the Future,
the book that had deeply impressed Dr. Attali,
and included it in this publication.

Lectures in the United States and Spain

Now, let me explain the background of the publication of
The Five Laws to Foresee the Future.

In 2007, I delivered a keynote lecture
at New School University in New York, USA.
The theme of that lecture was
Foreseeing the Future through Dialectic Thinking.

12

I spoke about
how we can foresee the future and
what we can foresee in the future.
I was pleased to receive kind words from many attendees
who expressed their desire for **the content of my lecture
to be published in English**.

The following year, in 2008,
I also delivered a keynote lecture at *iFest*, an event
which brings together innovators from various fields in Europe,
held in Barcelona, Spain.
Once again, I spoke about
Foreseeing the Future through Dialectic Thinking, and
I received encouraging words
from attendees and the organizer, Dr. Alfons Cornella,
expressing their wish for an English publication.

Consequently, I extensively expanded
the content of these lectures and published them
simultaneously in Japan and the US in 2008:

> Japanese edition: ***Mirai o yoken suru "itsutsu no hōsoku"***
> English edition: ***The Five Laws to Foresee the Future***

How to Read This Book, Recommended to Readers

In this way, this book,
Hiroshi Tasaka Talks about the Future of Humanity,
brings together the two essays born
out of the above two circumstances,
as well as one additional important essay,
into a single book composed of the following **three parts**:

> *Part I*   The **Twelve Insights** *to Foresee the Future*
> *Part II*   The **Five Laws** *to Foresee the Future*
> *Part III* The **Five Crises** *Facing Humanity*

Therefore,
readers who wonder, *how we can foresee the future*,
and are interested in my *method of foreseeing the future*,
are encouraged to start reading this book from
Part II: The Five Laws.

Next, readers who wonder, *what we can foresee in the future*,
and are interested in my *vision of the future*,
are encouraged to start reading this book from
Part I: The Twelve Insights.

Finally, there may be readers especially concerned with
the current state of the world, who wonder about the following:

> *Why is democracy retreating and autocracy spreading in the world?*
> *Why is capitalism widening the wealth gap in the world?*
> *Why are conflicts and wars frequent and nuclear war threats*
> *emerging in the world?*
> *Why do countries tend to turn from world economy*
> *to single-nation economy in the world?*
> *Why is there a return from scientific rationalism*
> *to religious mysticism in the world?*

Readers who have such questions
are encouraged to start reading this book from
Part III: The Five Crises.
Although it is a short discussion,
this **Part III** expresses my thoughts,
from a dialectical perspective,
on how to perceive and deal with these phenomena
that appear to be a *regression of history*.
This present age is a time when we are facing
numerous *problems without apparent solutions*;
it may literally be called an *era of confusion*.

14

In such a time,
many people wonder in their hearts the following questions:

What will the future of humanity be like going forward?
How can we cope with such a future?

It is my hope as the author that
this book may help people
by hinting at the answer to such questions.

It is my hope that
this book will be read by many people worldwide
as a *Japan-made* **method for foreseeing the future** *and*
a **vision of the future**.

February 17, 2023
Hiroshi Tasaka

Part I

The *Twelve Insights* to Foresee the Future

Chapter One

How Can We Foresee the Future?

— **Macroscopic View** by Dialectic —

How to Foresee the Future by Hegel's Dialectic

I have written over 100 books in the past 30 years.
Many of those have been books which offer insight into and
foresee the future of different aspects of our modern society
such as the revolution of the Internet and AI,
knowledge society, and capitalism.

To begin, therefore, I would like to start by discussing
methods of foreseeing the future in this Chapter One.
First, I will discuss the main points in Part I,
then I will go into more detail about these methods in Part II
under the subtitle, *The Five Laws to Foresee the Future*.

For the moment, I shall describe
the most crucial aspects of this method of foreseeing the future.
I believe that
*we cannot make **concrete predictions**, but*
*we can make **macroscopic foresights**.*

To conduct this **macroscopic foresight**,
I find *Hegel's Dialectic* to be extremely effective.
Dialectic underlies the logic and historical science of
18th-century German philosopher Georg Hegel,
but it was also used by Karl Marx,
the author of the historic work *The Capital* (*Das Kapital*),
to make his arguments regarding the development of capitalism
and the future of human society.

The Law of Development through *Spiral Process*

There are several laws of dialectic, but the most useful one is
the law of development through **spiral process**.

This law states that
change, development, progress, and evolution
proceed upward and around
as if climbing a spiral staircase.

That is, if we look at people
climbing a spiral staircase from the side,
they seem to be going up—
that is, they seem to be undergoing
progression and evolution.
On the other hand, if we look at them from above,
they are returning to their original place—
that is, they seem to be undergoing *revival and regression.*
In reality, however, you can be certain
they have arrived at a higher level than before
because it is a spiral staircase.
In other words, you can be certain
their revival and regression are accompanied by *new value.*

Consequently,
the law of development through **spiral process** means that,
as things in the world are
changing, developing, progressing, and evolving,
old and nostalgic things are revived
accompanied by new value.

Abundant Examples of the Spiral Development in the Online World

This is not mere *theory*, but *reality*
occurring in the world today.
In particular, we can find many things
indicative of the *spiral process* by considering
the developments brought about by the Internet revolution.

For example, *e-mail*, now used by nearly everyone in the world,
represents a revival of
the long-defunct culture of the *letter writing*.
Traditional letters take many days to be delivered and
are sent at a high cost.
E-mail, however, can be sent at no cost and
can reach people around the world instantly.
Furthermore, an e-mail can be sent simultaneously to
multiple recipients, and a record is maintained by all parties.
In this sense, e-mail can be seen as an example of
something nostalgic—the culture of letter writing—
being revived accompanied by **new value**.

Similarly, *online auctions* and *reverse auctions*
which have become common on the Internet,
are a revival of similar public sales that
once took place in town marketplaces.
However, while traditional *auctions* and *reverse auctions*
could only accommodate several hundreds of buyers at a time,
online auctions and reverse auctions can
accommodate millions of buyers worldwide.
This is none other than a **revival with new value added**.

In addition,
online education is a revival of *individualized learning*,
which adjusts to students' abilities, interests, and lifestyles.
This form of learning is like the old private tutor system of
Europe's aristocratic society and
the private temple school (*terakoya*) system of Edo Japan.

Our modern industrial society developed away from
these forms of education to heavily favor
a standardized form of **group education**.
With the emergence of online education, however,
individual learning has been revived, and
individual learners now have access to cutting-edge knowledge
from around the world.

Furthermore, the Internet revolution has given rise to
digital democracy—a revived form of *direct democracy*
once only commonly seen in small communities,
but now expanded to the national level.
In reality, there have been many instances of national policies
being influenced by people flocking to social media,
to express their opinions.

Now, there are many fields other than the Internet
in which we can see the **spiral process** at work.

For example,
the culture of *resource recycling*, which was valued in the past
when resources were extremely valuable,
is being reevaluated to resolve global environmental problems
that have come about after the age of mass production,
mass consumption and mass disposal.

In this way, we can see how
the law of development through **spiral process** can be a lens
through which we can look at modern society.
Looking through this lens,
we find that, in various fields and in various forms,
revivals of nostalgic things accompanied by new values
are taking place.

Law of Development through *Interpenetration of Opposites*

In addition, there is another important law in dialectic—
the law of development
through **interpenetration of opposites**.

This law states that
things which oppose and compete with each other
come to resemble each other.

In recent times, for example, *for-profit companies*
have begun to focus on **social contribution**
in the forms of *Corporate Social Responsibility (CSR)*
and *Sustainable Development Goals (SDGs)*.
On the other hand, *non-profit organizations*
have begun to emphasize **business profit**
to secure the sustainability of their social contributions
by evolving into *social entrepreneurs* and *social enterprises*.

In addition,
brokerage firms concentrating on direct financing and
banks concentrating on indirect financing
have begun to adopt each other's business practices,
evolving into **universal banks**.

Likewise, opposing political parties
have begun to incorporate the policies of their opponent.
Capitalists have learned and adopted
social welfare policies favored by socialists,
while *socialists* have learned and adopted
market principles touted by capitalists.

These are examples of the **interpenetration of opposites** and
it is none other than the most fundamental law of dialectic:
sublation (*aufheben* in German).

This **sublation** is the process by which
a **thesis** is met with an **antithesis** which is created to oppose it,
and through their **clash**
both **learn from** and **absorb each other**,
leading to a *final* **synthesis** on a higher plane.

There are **three laws** of dialectic other than those
discussed above, which you can read more about in Part II.

The Coming Paradigm Shifts

Now, if we look at the *future of humanity*
from a perspective of **dialectical laws**,
what can we foresee?

I offer the following examples, which I believe show
how the **spiral process** and **interpenetration of opposites**
will occur,
resulting in various *paradigm shifts*
in the future of human society.

1. The Internet revolution will cause
   a revival of nostalgic *voluntary economy*,
   which will merge with modern *monetary economy*,
   giving birth to a **new economic principle**.

2. Through the AI revolution, a regression will occur,
   shifting our cultural emphasis
   from *logical thinking* and *verbal expression*
   to *intuitive thinking* and *image-based expression*.

3. Through the emergence of complex systems society,
   there will be regression in various fields
   from a *mechanical system worldview*
   to a *living system worldview*.

4. *Religion* will come to adopt scientific theories, and
   science will proceed into the realm of
   deep spiritual revelations.
   As a result, there will be a merging of **religion** and **science**.

5. The *wisdom for living system and altruism* of
   Eastern civilization will merge with
   the *science, technology, and capitalism* of
   Western civilization, giving birth to a **New civilization**.

I shall further explore these **paradigm shifts**
throughout the following chapters.

Chapter Two

How Will Paradigm Technologies
Change Humanity's Future?
— The **Imagination** by Science Fiction—

The Age Requiring *Sci-fi Imagination*

In Chapter One, I discussed my use of *Hegel's dialectic*
as a method of foreseeing the future.
There is, however, one other method I use
when attempting to foresee the future.

It is what I call, *sci-fi imagination*.

I find that the *unrestrained imagination*
which forms the backbone of sci-fi novels and movies
provides me with *deep inspiration*
as I attempt to imagine the world of tomorrow.

I also believe that
sci-fi imagination will become more and more important
in coming years.
The reason for this is that, in the near future,
various *paradigm technologies* will emerge, develop quickly,
and spread throughout society.

What I mean by **paradigm technology** here is a technology
which fundamentally alters widely accepted *paradigms*
(or *fundamental frameworks*) of humanity and society.
Specifically, such technologies include
artificial intelligence technology, genetic engineering,
cloning technology, brain science, and surveillance technology.

To understand
how these technologies will change humanity and society,
however, it is not enough to study humanity's *past.*
For example, when cloning technology enables
the creation of a human being identical to their original,
what kind of impacts will this have
on human consciousness and culture?
We cannot answer this question by looking back to the past
because humanity has never experienced
such an event before.

It follows, therefore, that
what is required to foresee such a future is *sci-fi imagination*
which enables us to imagine the *unexperienced future*
that will be brought about
by scientific and technological advancements.
In fact, many futurists have stated
how sci-fi novels and movies are effective to foresee the future.

The Ability to Conduct *Thought Experiments*

Now, what exactly does the **sci-fi imagination** teach us
about the future?

Generally, it is said that sci-fi imagination is an effective tool
in foreseeing the *future of science and technology.*
Indeed, there are many things foreseen in science fiction
which have become a reality.
The **future technologies** that sci-fi writers,
beginning with Jules Verne and H. G. Wells,
depicted using only their imagination have all become reality:
spaceships, submarines, atomic bombs, genetic engineering,
communications satellites, and videophones.
The only exceptions seem to be technologies
for time travel, antigravity, and immortality.

The wise words of Jules Verne were true:
"Anything one man can imagine,
other men can make real."
And these words also describe
the history of science and technology.

However, in reality, true sci-fi imagination is
something which surpasses **technological imagination.**
This is because sci-fi imagination offers the *ability*
to conduct highly sophisticated **thought experiments**.
In other words, this is the *ability*
to conduct **psychological** *and* **social experiments**
with our imagination to foresee
how human consciousness and social culture
will be affected by radical new technologies.

Therefore, to conduct such **thought experiments**,
it is not enough just to have
a vast technological and scientific knowledge.
Without a deep understanding of **human psychology**
and sharp insight into **social culture**,
it is impossible to effectively wield the sci-fi imagination.

What I mean is that true sci-fi imagination represents
a synthesis of **technological imagination,**
psychological imagination, *and* **social imagination**,
and to foresee the future of human society,
we must integrate
our *knowledge of natural science and engineering*
with *knowledge of humanities science and social science.*

This process will require both an attempt to destroy the fences
that have separated these fields of study up until now,
as well as an attempt to create a new **21st Century Intellect**
which integrates these once segregated schools of thought.
Now, let us consider what kinds of **thought experiments**
are made possible by sci-fi imagination.

What Sci-fi Movies and Novels Deeply Teach Us

In the 2013 sci-fi film *Her*, for example, Theodore,
the protagonist, falls in love with his AI assistant Samantha.
Samantha reciprocates his love, but
as a supercomputer simultaneously serving 641 users,
her love for Theodore is actually a performance
meant to help him process the trauma of his divorce.
Now, even though Samantha's love is only a performance,
how would such a believable performance
move the human heart?
This is the **thought experiment** depicted by the film *Her.*

Next, let us consider a novel by **Kazuo Ishiguro**,
winner of the 2017 Nobel Prize in Literature.
In the novel *Never Let Me Go*, Ishiguro depicts a society
in which people use cloning technology
to have genetic copies of themselves created,
from which organs can be transplanted whenever they fall ill.
Moreover, this novel expresses with great sensitivity
the grief and sorrow that humans raised as clones
would experience in such a society.

In addition, the 2005 American sci-fi film
The Island realistically depicts, in a similar society,
the kinds of fictitious communities
that may be established for clones to preclude their despair.

Furthermore, let us consider **Philip K. Dick**'s sci-fi short story,
"We Can Remember It for You Wholesale" and
the film adaptation, *Total Recall.*
Both works realistically depict a future
in which brain science advancements allow us
to freely implant memories in our brains,
as well as the kind of society that may emerge,
and the psychological confusion people will fall into
if they cannot clearly distinguish
between *false memories* from *real memories*.

In this way,
the imagination underlying sci-fi novels and sci-fi movies
offers excellent inspirations
to foresee the future of humanity and society.
There is no end to such examples.

However, when attempting to gain insight into
the impact new technology will have
on the future of humanity using *sci-fi intellect,*
there is one thing we should deeply understand.

The Co-evolution of *Technology* and *Consciousness*

Namely, that
**technology is
an accelerator of the evolution of human consciousness**.

Over the course of our existence, we humans
have created the fields of science and technology,
and through their development
we have made our lives easier and our society richer.
However, when we look at so-called science and technology
from the overarching perspective of human history,
it can be said that
through the development of science and technology,
we have evolved our own **consciousness**.
In other words, throughout human history,
a process has been at work that may be called
the *mutual evolution of technology and consciousness*.

For example, with the *development of nuclear weapons*,
we humans were forced to become conscious of
the possibility of the *destruction of humanity*,
and when *the Apollo Program* gave us
the first ever pictures of the earth viewed from the moon,
in our minds emerged
what may be called *planetary consciousness*.

30

In addition, through the spread of the *Internet*,
we have been enabled to communicate instantly with
people all around the world via high-quality video,
profoundly changing our conception of **distance**.

At the same time, as MIT Professor **Sherry Turkle**
in her ***Life on the Screen*** points out,
most members of online communities,
where people can interact anonymously,
have come to sense within themselves the emergence of
hidden personalities and **multiple personalities**.

This tendency has become more and more clear in recent years
as a **virtual space** called the **Metaverse** has spread and
many people have created a **virtual persona** called an **avatar**
with which they participate in the virtual space,
engage in activities there,
and communicate with other **avatars**.

These are just a few examples of how the idea that
technology is
an accelerator of the evolution of consciousness
is incredibly important in considering
how technology will shape
human consciousness and social culture,
and how society will change in the future.

After all, it is ultimately our *human consciousness*
that will shape the *society of the future*.

Chapter Three

How to Cope with a *Highly Complex System Society*

— A Social System with a **Will** of its Own—

Enterprises, Markets, and Society as *Complex Systems*

When foreseeing the future of human society,
I believe there is one important **question** we need to ask.

That is,
through the exercise of human will, to what degree
*are we able to **control** the social system in which we live?*

The reason we need to ask this question is that,
currently, our society exists as a highly *complex system*,
and that the system is still growing more complex.

In our modern society, great progress has been made
through the information revolution,
with the Internet revolution at its center,
and with this progress the *interconnectivity*
between individual humans and between organizations
has rapidly increased within enterprises, markets and society.
Moreover, globalization has opened the world,
leading to the spread of networks formed with outside entities
and strengthening this interconnectedness.
As a result, modern enterprises, markets, and society
all behave as *highly complex systems*.

Now, how exactly does a **highly complex system** behave?

The Behavior of a *Living System*

In a word,
*it behaves as a **living system***.
This is because, as the ***complexity*** of a system increases,
it begins to exhibit the following properties:

emergence and self-organization;
ecosystem formation;
evolution and co-evolution; and
the butterfly effect,

all of which are properties of a **living system**.

The first of these traits, ***emergence** and **self-organization**,*
are *properties by which a system will,*
naturally and without deliberate external direction,
form its own internal order and structure.

For example, modern markets,
without a ***de jure standard*** established
by the government or a public body,
will nonetheless form their own ***de facto standard***
as the result of free competition.
There are many examples of this happening around the world.
The Windows operating system and
common media formats such as VHS, DVD, and Blu-ray,
are examples of **de facto standards** which came into being
through the ***process of emergence*** within the market.

Concerning ***ecosystem formation**,*
we can see how the excellent ***business ecosystem***
that formed in Silicon Valley in the US.
is what gave rise to many start-ups emerging in that region.
Furthermore, modern market strategy is
not focused on a competition of **products**,
but rather one of ***product ecosystems***;
in the previous example of Windows and VHS, for example,

these products did not win out in the market
due to **superiority of product**,
but rather ***superiority of product ecosystem***.

Furthermore, regarding ***evolution*** and ***co-evolution***,
we can look to the ways in which
customer awareness *and* ***company policy*** co-evolve.
As customer awareness of environmental issues increases,
customers begin to purchase products
that are made with the environment in mind.
As a result, companies begin to create
such products for customers.
Conversely, as companies begin to offer such products,
the awareness of customers is altered.
This is a form of ***co-evolution***.

Furthermore, as investors turn more towards **SDG investment**,
companies also begin to focus on **SDGs**; and, conversely,
as companies start branding themselves as ***SDG companies***,
investors become more likely to support such companies.
This is another form of co-evolution.

The Threat and Hope of the *Butterfly Effect*

Now, what about the ***butterfly effect***?

This concept,
common in the nonlinear science of ***chaos theory***,
is derived from the saying,
if a butterfly flutters its wings in Beijing,
a hurricane occurs in New York;
in other words,
a small fluctuation in an insignificant corner of a system
can have huge consequences to the overall system.

A negative example of the butterfly effect is
the *global economic crisis* brought about

34

by the Lehman Shock in 2008.
In this case, it was the failure of loans
in a corner of the world (the US housing market)
that led to a worldwide economic crisis.

On the other hand,
a positive example would be the company Google.
The search engine developed by researchers
Sergey Brin and **Larry Page**
in a small corner of the world (Stanford University),
radically changed how we handle information in the world.

At the same time,
Steve Jobs' iPod and iPhone dramatically changed
the world's way of enjoying music and of communicating.
Also, microfinance,
pioneered by a Bangladeshi man named **Muhammad Yunus**,
greatly altered the way
needy people around the world can access financial aid.

In this way, the *butterfly effect* has become stronger than
ever in our society as a ***highly complex system***;
and because of this,
it is possible for the financial crisis of a single country
to draw the whole world into economic crisis,
but also for a single entrepreneur or social entrepreneur
to fundamentally change the world.

We can see from the above examples
how modern society, which exists as a **highly complex system**,
is a ***living system*** that exhibits
emergence and self-organization, ecosystem formation,
evolution and co-evolution, and the butterfly effect.

If so, what exactly happens
when a social system becomes more and more
like a **living system**?

Difficult to Predict and _Difficult to Control_

We face two problems.

One is that _it becomes difficult to **predict** such behavior._
Specifically, the **butterfly effect**,
which allows for small fluctuations
to change the behavior of the whole system,
makes **prediction** of the behavior extremely difficult.

The other problem is that _it becomes difficult_
to exert **control** over the behavior of the system.
Specifically, as the processes of
emergence and **self-organization** become stronger,
intentional _control, management, and manipulation_
of the social system become more and more difficult.
Finally, as emergence and self-organization,
ecosystem formation, and co-evolution gain strength,
the social system itself _exhibits behavior_
which seems to suggest that it has a **will** of its own.

For example, why is it that
bureaucracy only seems to grow uncontrollably?
Why is it that the military-industrial complex causes war?
Why is it that
modern capitalism continues to widen the wealth gap?

The reason for all of these is
not that individual people or organizations
are deliberately causing them,
but that the social system itself is causing them
through its own _**self-movement**_.

Considering this, is it therefore impossible
to intentionally control **a society as a highly complex system**
which seems to have its own **will**?

The Technique of *Intentional Emergence*

The answer to this question can be found in a concept
developed at *the Santa Fe Institute* in the US.,
a leader in complex systems research.

That concept is
intentional emergence.

The idea is that
*a **highly complex system** cannot be subjected to*
*intentional **control**;*
*however, **emergence** of the system can be*
intentionally encouraged.

In other words,
while a social system cannot be controlled or manipulated
*as though it were a **mechanical system**,*
*as a **living system***
its emergence, self-organization, evolution, and co-evolution
can be encouraged to move in a desirable direction.

Now, what is the method by which we achieve this?

Laws and Ethics for Determining
the Behavior of a *Complex System*

To answer this question, we need an understanding of
the fundamental nature of **complex systems.**
Namely, one must understand that,
while a complex system's behavior cannot be
externally controlled,
its entire behavior is determined by the behavioral rules of
***individual agents** which comprise the system.*

This means that, in terms of a social system,
*one must change the behavioral rules of **individual people***
to change the behavior of the overall society.

Moreover, it follows that,
to promote the emergence and self-organization of society
to move in a desirable direction,
laws** and **ethics, which represent **behavioral rules**, will surely
come to hold an even greater significance than ever before.

Specifically, **ethics** are particularly important
from the viewpoint of **autonomy**,
and in that sense ***philanthropy** and **altruism*** will become
extremely important in the coming age
to changing a society as a **highly complex system**.

Mechanical System Worldview and *Living System Worldview*

Moreover,
as our social system becomes a **highly complex system**,
developing more and more as a **living system**,
the conventional *mechanical system worldview*
will reach its limit.
The **mechanical system worldview** is a worldview
by which we see society, markets, and enterprises
as **mechanical systems**.

For example, practices such as
the business reform method called **re-engineering**,
the way of **market manipulation**, and
the drawing of **blueprints** or **designs** of society
will all come up against a wall.

At that point, the **mechanical system worldview**
which dominated the 20th century will wane, and
the *living system worldview* will come to prominence
in the 21st century.

What it means
for the **living system worldview** to become important is
that there will then be a demand for
wisdom with which we can cope with systems
that seem to have a **life** and **will** of their own,
wisdom that perceives businesses, markets, and society
as **living systems**.

Traditional Wisdom Existing throughout the World

If so, where can we find such *wisdom*?

We should not search for it
in cutting-edge complex systems research
being conducted in places like the Santa Fe Institute;
rather, I believe we should seek it
in the ancient wisdom of our respective countries.

The reason I believe this is that,
in every country there was once a living system worldview
that came with it,
but we lost sight of it in the process of modernization;
and now,
in the midst of the information revolution and globalization,
this worldview is ready to be revived through the process of
spiral development of dialectic.

I will discuss
the meaning of this revival in more detail in Part II.

Chapter Four

Where is the World Headed after This Pandemic?

— Humanity's **Altruism Test** —

The Needs for Realizing a *Para-pandemic Society*

The novel coronavirus known as COVID-19
has ravaged the world since 2020.
But when this pandemic is finally over,
what sort of society should we humans build up?

First, what we must initially prepare ourselves for is
the fact that new viruses will come up
which cause worldwide pandemics over and over again.

It follows, therefore, that humanity must build
a sustainable society that,
should a pandemic occur at any time and in any form,
can secure the safety and peace of mind of its people,
as well as ensure that
economic activities are uninterrupted.

I would call such a society a *para-pandemic society*.

My Vision of a *Dual Mode Society*

Now, what kind of society would this be?

I would like to propose one vision of society.

*That is a **dual mode society**.*

What I mean by this is,
just as many automobiles these days have *dual modes*,
being able to switch between **sport mode**
which focuses on comfort over fuel consumption,
and **eco mode** which minimizes fuel consumption,
society going forward must develop an *economy mode*
which, as the default, focuses on economic efficiency
with little concern for infectious diseases,
and a *safety mode* which, during pandemics,
focuses on minimizing the spread of disease;
and we must develop a system
by which society can easily and quickly switch
from **economy mode** to **safety mode** in times of emergency.
This is what I mean by a *dual mode society*.

The True Meaning of *New Normal*

Now, what does society look like in **safety mode**?

The perfect example of this is a phrase that was used
all over the world at the beginning of the COVID-19 pandemic:
new normal.
However, this simple phrase has been often interpreted
in a narrow sense by governments to mean a
new way of life or *new manners for everyday life and work*
which is meant to help society continue running smoothly
during a pandemic by preventing the spread of disease
through limiting outings, contact between people,
large gatherings of people, and movement in general.

However, *new normal* in essence has the meaning of
a *new society* that is able to promote
disease prevention and economic activity
in the long-term during a pandemic.

So the basic premise of new normal is *sustainability*

which is necessary to realize a *para-pandemic society*.
In other words, *new normal* means a *new paradigm*
which governments must strive to realize in all fields
from science, technology, government, and administration
to medicine, welfare, education, and culture.
Such efforts will build up a society
that is able to withstand any sort of pandemic.

For example, during the COVID-19 pandemic,
remote work and work-from-home became quite common.
Likewise, restaurants began offering more takeout and
delivery options and many online services also expanded.

We must not let these changes become simply
temporary stop-gap measures
which make economic sacrifices.

Rather, through
the adoption of cutting-edge technologies,
the establishment of new systems, and
the nurturing of a mature culture,
we must make these
sustainable measures
which thoroughly address economic considerations.

We must enact changes in various societal fields, including:
New societal systems
New business models
New labor models, and
New lifestyle habits.

Then, for the first time, governments will be able to realize
a *dual mode society* able to switch quickly
from *economic mode* to *safety mode*
based on the new normal brought about
when a pandemic occurs.

Transitioning to the New Normal Occurring in All Fields

Now, in order to realize this *para-pandemic society*,
what is the *new normal* towards which
the government must promote transitions
in various fields such as
science and technology, government and administration,
economics and business, and education and culture?
Allow me to make some suggestions.

Firstly, in the field of *science and technology*,
it goes without saying that
the development and dissemination of
virus-prevention measures, viral testing methods, and
viral treatments is important.
But to realize this **para-pandemic society**,
it is vital that
we also develop and disseminate a *technical system*
*that will become the core of a **dual mode society***.

That is a technical system called
contactless technology,
which *minimizes* **contact between and movement of people**.

To be specific, this is a group of technologies including
the Internet, remote technologies, virtual reality, robotics, AI,
face and voice recognition, automated driving, and drones,
which will become the central industrial technologies
in the age of *the Fourth Industrial Revolution*.
In other words, to the government,
policies to realize a *para-pandemic society* are also
policies to accelerate *the Fourth Industrial Revolution*,
and furthermore, they are policies
that will help grow *new industry* in various fields of society
through the development and spread of
these *new industrial technologies*.

If this is the case,
governments must not become too focused on
the current policies for combating infectious diseases.
Rather, they should clearly uphold the following vision:
Policies to realize a para-pandemic society are
policies to promote new industry growth.

New Normal in the Field of
Government and Administration

Secondly, in the field of *government and administration*,
the *voting system* must first be changed.
That is, to avoid many people being unable to vote
due to stay-at-home restrictions during pandemics,
we must adopt *remote voting* policies
by which voters can vote by mail or online.

Also, based on our experience with
the COVID-19 pandemic response,
we learned just how limited a *centralized government* can be
in both speed and effectiveness.
Therefore, in the future,
we must move towards a *decentralized regional government*
in order to transfer greater authority and resources
to **local governing bodies**
which can more quickly and effectively implement measures
to prevent the spread of diseases.

Furthermore,
to prevent *capital functions* from stalling during pandemics,
they too should be *regionally decentralized*.

New Normal in the Field of *Economics and Business*

Thirdly, in the field of *economics and business*,
we must support the forming

during normal times of ***employee share*** contracts
between ***businesses which need fewer workers***
and ***business which need more workers*** during a pandemic.
There are already partnerships forming between the fields of
tourism and agriculture, taxi and delivery companies, etc.,
but governments should be acting to support the spread of
such partnerships to a greater variety of businesses.

Also, from the perspective of individuals,
it will become a new normal
for a person to hold ***multiple occupations***
in order to ensure their income does not dry up
during a pandemic.
This too should be supported by governments
through employment systems and policies.

New Normal in the Field of *Education and Culture*

Fourthly, in the field of ***education and culture***,
it will first be necessary to spread ***online learning***.
However, this should not merely be
a **desperate alternative measure** used
when a novel coronavirus forces schools to close their doors.
Rather, governments should *use* the *COVID-19 crisis*
as an opportunity to overhaul our education systems.
Specifically, we should use cutting-edge technology
to spread ***online video workshop*** which offers students
hands-on experience which normal classes could not
through realistic video workshops.

The reason for this is that
as ***the Fourth Industrial Revolution*** proceeds
and AI becomes more widespread,
experiential knowledge
learned through real experience and video workshops
will become more important than simple
book knowledge learned from textbooks and reference books.

Furthermore, in the near future
this experiential method of education and learning will become
vital to human resources development strategies for states.

Also, as I will explain in the next chapter,
"Artificial Intelligence Revolution,"
what is demanded of human resources will change dramatically
in the age of **the Fourth Industrial Revolution**,
and because of this, *reskilling* of human resources
will become more and more important.
Therefore, governments should support efforts
to develop online language and technical courses, etc.,
that can effectively utilize people's time at home
when they are restricted due to pandemics,
by having them work on **skills development**.

The COVID-19 Crisis is a Perfect Opportunity for Social Reform

As I have explained above,
in order to realize a *para-pandemic society* moving forward,
governments must have a clear vision and strategy
to facilitate the transition to various forms of *new normal*
in many fields such as
*science and technology, government and administration,
economics and business, and education and culture.*

However,
these changes should not simply be *defensive reform*.
Governments should take the COVID-19 crisis as
an *opportunity to create a new society*, and
an *opportunity to develop new industry*.
And as such,
they should make these changes *aggressive reform*.

That is, governments must not fall into
the trap of focusing only on the problems facing them

during the COVID-19 pandemic,
but rather, they should create
a vision of a post-pandemic *new society* and create
clear national strategies to make that vision a reality.

The Definitive Difference
between *Pandemic Crisis* and *Economic Crisis*

Now, up until this point
I have focused on offering some suggestions about
the kinds of *visions* and *policies*
that governments should promote
in order to realize a *para-pandemic society*.
However, now I would like to
broaden our horizons and bring up problems
from the *perspective of humanity* in general.

Actually, to create a true **para-pandemic society**,
it will not be enough to simply promote transitions to
a **new normal** in various fields.

That is because, to create a true **para-pandemic society**,
we must deepen our understanding of
the *concepts of **philanthropy** and **altruism***
which are the underpinnings of human society.

The reason for this is that the *pandemic crises*
humanity will face time and again in the future
will be utterly different from the *economic crises*
that we have faced up until now.

That is to say, up until now,
we have overcome economic crises
by sacrificing *the economically weak* (i.e. *the poor*),
despite government promises to **save the weak**.
While there have been huge sacrifices among the poor,
including high rates of

unemployment, bankruptcy, broken homes, and suicide,
the economically strong (i.e. *the rich*) have come out of
economic crises with relatively few losses.

However, pandemic crises are different from economic crises
in that we may be unable to overcome it
by the old way of *sacrificing the weak*.

The *Solidarity Test* Given to Humanity

There are three reasons for this.

Firstly,
with a virus, so long as even one person is infected,
there is risk of the *disease spreading* or of an *outbreak*
which would put both rich and poor equally at risk of infection.

Secondly,
when the disease spreads or an outbreak of infections occurs,
it can *break down the medical infrastructure* of
a society as a whole,
resulting in a loss in access to medical care
not only for the poor, but also for the rich.

And finally, the third reason is that,
as laborers among the lower classes
become unable to work due to infection,
there is a net loss of laborers called *essential workers*,
who support societal infrastructure;
due to such loss, many of society's faculties
will cease to function, resulting in significant losses
even to the livelihood of the upper classes.

That is to say, pandemic crises, in contrast to economic crises,
will require us to develop a social system
that gives appropriate medical care to the economically weak,
an *inclusive humanitarian social system*

48

that will not abandon the poor;
failing to do so will keep us from overcoming such crises.

Czech economist Tomas Sedlacek describes this idea, saying,
*"Pandemics are **solidarity tests** for humanity,"*
and I must agree.

To put it another way, this can be called
an ***altruism test***
given to the entirety of humanity.

What is *Rational Altruism*?

However, such ***altruism*** must not be understood
as a concept in conflict with **self-interest**.

I am not talking about an altruism
predicated on ***self-sacrifice***, or
sacrificing oneself for the sake of another.

The altruism I am talking about is one by which
giving one's utmost effort for another is
in one's own best interest.

That is, I believe what humanity will need going forward is
not ***self-sacrificing altruism***,
which conceives **altruism** and **self-interest**
as opposite to each other,
but rather ***rational altruism***
which is a dialectic ***sublation*** (*aufheben*) of
altruism and self-interest.

Altruism is Self-interest

Actually, Buddhism,
which forms the basis of Eastern Thought,
has long held that
self-interest is altruism, and altruism is self-interest.

And in Japan there is an old phrase that goes,
compassion is not only for the sake of others.

I believe we should conceive of true **altruism**
not as the *dichotomic opposite of self-interest*,
but as *integrated and sublated with* **self-interest**.

Because of this, the *inclusive humanitarian social system*
I mentioned before, *which*
chooses to save rather than abandon the weak in society,
should be built up based on this idea of **rational altruism**.

Rational Altruism that Transcends Generations

Furthermore, the reason that *rational altruism* is needed
is not only to cope with pandemics.

In order to solve the great number of serious crises
humanity faces in the 21st century,
from global warming, environmental destruction,
and dwindling resources to energy crises, water shortages,
and food supply crises,
the idea of **rational altruism** requires us to consider that
prioritizing the interests of future generations is
also in the best interest of the current generation.

In reality,
there is an explosion of young people all around the world
protesting the governments of the **current generation**,
which are failing to enforce policies to reduce
carbon emissions which will gravely harm *future generations*.
If this continues,
the *gap and animosity between generations* will deepen,
which will certainly not lead to a good future
for the current generation
as they come into their retirement years.

Rational Altruism **and** *Rational Intellect*

Now, what is needed to spread this idea of *rational altruism*?

Originally, this idea should have at its heart
a sense of philanthropy and compassion,
ethics and morality.
In reality, however, more important than these things is a
grasp on reality and foresight based on rational intellect.

This is because
we humans are distracted by quick profits and, not realizing
that we are likely to lose the precious profits in the future,
to run head-first into *self-destructive self-interest.*
The cause of this is
a *failure to properly understand the reality before our eyes*
based on scientific findings, and
an *inability to understand what will happen in the future*
based on objective information.

What I mean by this is that it is not only
distracting **self-interest** which obstructs
the dissemination of *rational altruism*, but also
anti-intellectualism, *which disavows* **rational intellect.**

51

An example of this is *Trumpism* in the US,
which refutes the scientific discussion of COVID-19
and reasonable measures to limit its spread.

If so, in the coming age, who will it be that
spreads **rational altruism** around the world?

The Age in Which *Religion* and *Science* Will Join Forces

Looking back in history,
we see that the greatest advocates of **altruism**
for the poor and socially disadvantaged, who most often
preached the virtues of philanthropy and compassion,
as well as ethics and morality, were *religions*.

However, I believe in coming years it will be *science*
that is in the best position to objectively understand reality,
foresee the future, and promote *rational altruism*.

In this context, I believe that **religion** and **science**,
which up until now have been conceived of as opposites,
will join forces to preach
the importance of **rational altruism** to the world.

I shall discuss this in more detail
in *Part III: The Five Crises Facing Humanity*.

52

Chapter Five

What Will the *AI Revolution* Bring about?

— Illusion of **Basic Income** —

Mass Unemployment **Brought about by AI**

Now, let us consider
how the *artificial intelligence (AI)* technology,
which is now rapidly developing,
will change human society in the future.

Originally, AI is meant to allow society to offer services
that are more efficient, convenient, and pleasant
than ever before, to drastically raise economic productivity,
and moreover to allow us to choose the most optimal solutions
to the various problems facing society.
In these ways, AI is an outstanding technology.

However, where there is *light* there is also *shadow*, and
AI, too, has a *dark side*.

I say this because,
as this technology is developed and spreads throughout society,
it will come to do more and more *knowledge work*
which humans have traditionally been charged with;
and this will bring about a serious social problem,
that is, a *great loss of jobs among knowledge workers.*

Specifically,
AI has an overwhelming advantage over humans in the areas of
logical thinking and *knowledge management,*
meaning that a majority of knowledge work in these *two areas*
will one day be given to AI instead of humans.

In fact, AI have already come to take over some of the work traditionally done by humans in ***intellectual professions***, such as bankers, securities dealers, lawyers, accountants, doctors, and pharmacists—work that can only be done using ***logical thinking*** and ***knowledge management***.

Because of this, a certain accounting organization in Japan, concerned that ***half of the traditional accountant's work will be taken over by AI***
and hoping to find ways to cope with this crisis,
is considering what abilities accountants need to improve to make sure they are not replaced by AI in the future.

However, it is unfortunate that
the number of organizations and corporations
that feel this is a real crisis are still few.
Concern for the *mass unemployment to be caused by AI has yet to spread throughout society as a whole.*
Furthermore, governments, corporations, and individuals are all blissfully ignorant of the mass unemployment
that the AI revolution is sure to bring about;
they are carried away by a *groundless optimism*
that allows them to ignore this imminent crisis.

***Intuition* and *Wisdom* of Humanity**

If so, as the AI revolution continues its rapid progression, what abilities should we acquire to keep AI from replacing us in the coming age?
Moreover, what abilities should governments and corporations help their human resources to develop?

The answer to these questions is clear.

The answer will not be
logical thinking or **knowledge management**,
abilities AI excels in, but rather

those abilities which humans perform better than AI—
intuitive judgement and *wisdom management*.

These are the abilities we must acquire and develop.
In this context,
knowledge is *that which can be expressed in words*, or,
to put it another way,
that which can be learned from *books and documents*.
Wisdom, on the other hand, is
that which cannot be expressed in words, or
that which can only be understood
through *physical experience*.

In other words, this **wisdom** is
what scientific philosopher **Michael Polanyi** referred to
as *tacit knowing* (often called *tacit knowledge*)
in his book *The Tacit Dimension*, and
it is an area in which humans have a great advantage over AI.

On top of this, the ability of *intuitive judgement* is also
something that must be learned
through the accumulation of physical experience,
making humans superior to AI in this area.

Intuitive Decision-Making Demonstrated by AI

In reality, however,
AI have taken the first steps toward attaining this ability,
and are already beginning to replace humans
in some aspects of this area.

For example, *taxi drivers*, with long years of experience and
expert knowledge of local roads and traffic tendencies,
have traditionally had an advantage over other drivers,
being able to judge intuitively
at what times and on what streets
they could most easily find customers.

56

Taxi companies in Japan, however,
have begun to use big data and AI
to give even new drivers directions on where to go
and they have actually increased sales.
Also, *American police departments* use big data and AI
to know where, on what day, and at what time
crime is likely to be committed,
in order to instruct police to patrol specific areas
to increase arrest rates and lower crime rates.
Such know-how used to be something
only *experienced police officers* knew intuitively.

In this way, the work that AI can take from humans
does not stop at **simple knowledge work**, but
is expanding into the realm of **sophisticated knowledge work**
required for intuitive judgement.
And this is a great threat to the future of knowledge workers.

Three Abilities Which AI Cannot Take Over

If so, what specific **abilities are there that
only humans can demonstrate and that
AI will be unable to perform well enough to replace us**
in the coming age?

In the past, I was a member of the Global Agenda Council of
the World Economic Forum (Davos Forum).
During our meetings,
we had a broad range of discussions about these problems.
Through these discussions,
many authorities have come to agree that
the following **three abilities** are not replaceable by AI.

   (1) Hospitality
   (2) Management
   (3) Creativity

However, what we did not discuss at length is
what specific component abilities contribute to
*the above **three abilities**, or*
how exactly we should acquire and further develop
***these abilities** in the future.*
Therefore, I would like to briefly offer my thoughts on this.

The Two Powers of *Hospitality*

Firstly, with regards to ***hospitality***,
AI will easily replace humans
in areas based on ***verbal communication***,
such as reception and information services.
Therefore, humans must acquire more sophisticated abilities
in the field of hospitality.
In order to do so,
the following ***two powers*** will be essential in the coming age.

First is the ***power to conduct non-verbal communication***.
In other words, we need to improve our ability
to listen to the silent voice of customers, coworkers, etc.,
and grasp what they are feeling.
Also, we must develop our power to communicate
that which transcends words,
such as warmth and friendliness towards others.

Second is the ***power of deep interpersonal empathy***.
This is the ability to think about
things from another's perspective, and by doing so,
to feel what they feel and empathize with them.
This power is essential to demonstrating
the most sophisticated level of non-verbal communication.
Needless to say,
the ***power to conduct non-verbal communication*** and
the ***power of deep interpersonal empathy***
can never be replaced by AI.

58

The Two Powers of *Management*

Next, with regard to *management*,
AI will replace workers in tasks such as
financial management, materials management,
human resource management, and project management,
areas in which AI abilities are expected to
exceed those of humans in the future.
Consequently,
humans will need to take on more advanced management tasks
that cannot be replaced by AI.
Specifically,
the following *two powers* play a key role in this area.

First is the *power to conduct growth management*.
This is the ability of
an organization's manager or team leader to support members
in the development of their skills and professional growth;
fundamental to this power is the *coaching power*.

Second is the *power to employ psychological management*.
This is the ability to support
the recovery of organization members in distress
who are suffering psychological problems
rising from interpersonal relationships or other issues;
fundamental to this power is the *counseling power*.

Both the *power to conduct growth management*
and *power to employ psychological management*,
which can never be replaced by AI,
will be extremely important for managers and leaders
in the workplaces of the advanced knowledge society to come.

The Two Powers of *Creativity*

Regarding the final ability, *creativity*,
AI will never be able to substitute humans

with genius-level abilities who are capable of
the **invention of innovative technology**,
the **proposition of novel designs**, etc.
Meanwhile, such abilities are out of reach for most individuals.
So then, what constitutes **creativity** that
everyone can demonstrate in the age of AI?
The answer is the following *two powers.*

First is
the *power to perform collective intelligence management*.
This is the power to promote
the process by which organization members get together,
share their knowledge and wisdom, and hold discussions,
leading to the *emergence* of new knowledge and wisdom.
There are two powers which enable
the power to perform collective intelligence management.
One is the *power to convey vision*, or
the ability of a manager or a leader to express their vision
to organization members in a way that excites them.
The other is the *power to conduct ego management*, or
the ability to create a space
where members can transcend their individual egos
to cooperate with each other.

Second is
the *power to realize new ideas within an organization*.
To demonstrate this power requires
not only the *proposal* of a new idea,
but also the explanation and conveyance of its appeal,
the skillful persuasion of senior staff, and
the smooth development of the idea through the organization,
culminating in its *realization*.
In fact,
creativity that is truly required in a corporation or organization
involves much more than the *power to propose new ideas*.
It also requires
the *power to perform collective intelligence management*
and the *power to realize new ideas within an organization*.

60

These are **two powers** that can never be demonstrated by AI
in place of humans.

The *Six Powers* Only Humans Can Demonstrate

In this way, the following *six powers* can be considered
sophisticated abilities which only humans can demonstrate,
and which are impossible for AI to attain in the age to come.

> *(1) Power of Non-verbal Communication*
> *(2) Power of Deep Interpersonal Empathy*
> *(3) Power of Growth Management*
> *(4) Power of Psychological Management*
> *(5) Power of Collective Intelligence Management*
> *(6) Power to Realize New Ideas Within an Organization*

Consequently, during the AI revolution in coming years,
governments and corporations will need to
support citizens and employees
as they work to attain and develop these abilities
to prevent the mass unemployment of knowledge workers.
Furthermore, it will be extremely important
for even individuals to improve such abilities
to keep AI from taking their jobs.

The Illusion of *Basic Income*

On the other hand, however,
there is an argument circulating around the world
for an optimistic policy with regard to
the potential mass unemployment of knowledge workers.

That is, the policy called ***basic income***.

Specifically, to prevent AI-related unemployment,
this policy has been proposed to

implement high corporate taxes,
taking a portion of the massive profits gained
by corporations that introduce and use AI
to greatly increase productivity, and allocating those funds
to guarantee a minimum yearly income for citizens.

Of course, if it were actually implemented, such a policy would
offer a certain level of relief to AI-related unemployment.
Under the *current system of capitalism,* however,
there is no way such a policy could be implemented.
This is because any social democratic policy
based on heavy corporate taxation to fund public welfare,
even if the policy is heavily advocated, will be opposed by
big corporations and corporate associations which have
great financial influence over controlling political parties,
and which will want to stop
any increase to their corporate taxes.

Therefore, unless we fundamentally transform
our current system of capitalism,
any **basic income policy**, no matter how well it is advertised,
is nothing more than an **illusion**.

The *True Nature* of the Technology Called AI

Furthermore,
supposing a basic income system could be implemented,
we need to seriously consider whether such a system—
one which, beyond merely offering a safety net
for those in economic straits, would mean that
the government supports the livelihood of individuals,
even if they don't work—
is truly a superior system or not.

The reason for this is that **work** offers something called
the **joy factor of work**
which is derived from the satisfaction of customers,

contributing to society, etc.
Specifically, as mentioned above,
the work we humans will do in the age of AI
will be highly sophisticated work that only humans can do;
work which differs from the **hard labor** of
the previous industrial society;
work that is highly sophisticated, brings us deep joy,
and may at times be called **art**.

And if we consider this,
it becomes apparent that governments and corporations
have a fundamental responsibility
to conduct **skills development education** that
will help those in danger of losing their jobs
among the mass unemployment in the age of the AI,
and to have people work in areas
requiring **sophisticated work** that AI cannot do,
offering both good salaries and
a greater sense of the **joy factor of work**.

Finally, it goes without saying that
such a policy of ability development and training
would enhance our consciousness,
expanding our possibilities and leading to
the evolution of human society to an even higher stage.

That is, AI is not a technology that will make humans obsolete,
and neither is it a technology that will come to control humans.

It is none other than
a *technology that will form the foundation of a stage*
on which humans can demonstrate
their highest-level abilities.

Let us not forget that AI technology is
an **accelerator of the evolution of human consciousness**,
as I mentioned in Chapter Two.

Chapter Six

What Will *Genetic Engineering* Bring about?

— The Nightmare of a **Biological Class Society** —

The *Light* and *Dark* Sides of Genetic Engineering

Now, like AI technology,
the field of **genetic engineering** is rapidly developing.
If so, what sort of influence will this technology have
on the future of humanity?

First of all, if we look at the *light* side of genetic engineering,
it is possible that the development of this technology
will free humanity from the shackles of various diseases.
It may even lead to
the development of *breakthroughs in medicine*
that will be able to combat diseases,
such as cancer, that have caused countless years' suffering and
brought death to so many people—diseases
that have until now been considered **incurable diseases**.
Also, by applying this technology to animals,
we may be able to develop new methods
in the field of *organ transplantation*.
Moreover, by genetically manipulating plants,
we can create crops that are resistant to harsh changes
in weather and produce bigger yields,
which are expected to be pivotal in solving *food crises*.

In this way, there are many positive aspects to
the **light** side of genetic engineering.
At the same time, there is also a terrible *dark* side to
this technology which harbors the possibility of
bringing about the ruin of humanity in the future.

For example, it is impossible to deny the possibility that
a virus could be artificially created through genetic engineering
to be extremely contagious and lethal,
leading to a worldwide explosion of infections and
causing a pandemic that would eventually
bring about the ruin of humanity.
We have all felt the reality of this danger
through our experience of the COVID-19 pandemic
that started in 2020.

Designer Baby Technology

Now, I would like to take this opportunity
to discuss what greatly interests me
regarding the *contrast of* **light** *and* **dark**
in the field of genetic engineering.

That is, something called ***designer baby*** technology.

This technology would allow for the use of
genetic manipulation to the ***fertilized eggs of humans***
to benefit the unborn child
by removing genetic characteristics that
may contribute to certain diseases, and
by ensuring that the child has genetic characteristics that
contribute to physical and intellectual excellence.

The **light** side of such a technology goes without saying,
but the **dark** side does come with problems.

If so, what exactly are the problems?

The Emergence of a *Hopelessly Polarized Society*

To give one example, the American sci-fi film *Gattaca* (1997)
symbolically depicts the types of problems that
the **dark** side of such technology will bring about.

This movie tells the story of Anton,
a man genetically manipulated to excel
physically and intellectually,
and his older brother Vincent,
who was born without such genetic manipulations.
In the society these two brothers live in,
humans are categorized as
valid, or those who have undergone genetic manipulation, and
invalid, or those who have not undergone such manipulation;
in such a society, invalids are considered to have lesser abilities
and are therefore discriminated against
and barred from high-level jobs.

Gattaca is a heartwarming story in which
Vincent the invalid fabricates his identity,
overcomes his physical and intellectual handicaps
by sheer force of will, and
eventually proves his worth in the world of the valids
by being chosen to be an astronaut.
However, if such designer baby technology were
actually implemented in our society,
unfortunately it is almost certain that
such heartwarming stories would not come to pass;
rather, it is much more likely that
we would only create a *hopelessly polarized society*.

A Society in Which *Wealth Gaps* Will Become *Ability Gaps*

The reason for this is that, as has always been the case,
those who are able to benefit from
such cutting-edge medical technologies
are only those who can afford them—that is, the **wealthy**.
It doesn't matter
how groundbreaking this designer baby technology is;
as long as it entails a high cost,
society will discriminate between the **wealthy children**
who are genetically bestowed with superior abilities
and the **poor children**
who couldn't improve their abilities genetically.

Of course, such ability inequality may be solved
if national governments take on the expense and
apply designer baby technology to all citizens.
However, if we look at the state of the world,
the reality is that *wealth gaps* still exist in every country, and
those gaps are only widening.
Furthermore,
there is not always enough government support for the poor,
and the hard fact of the matter is that
the *children of the poor* are not being sufficiently educated
causing an even more distinct gap in ability
compared to the *children of the wealthy*.

Considering this, it is clear that
the actual implementation of designer baby technology
would drastically widen the already existing ability gap.

The Strongest *Class Society*

If so, what exactly would happen
if genetic engineering actually made this technology a reality,
resulting in a definitive ability gap
between wealthy and poor children?

The answer is that
it would give rise to a *new class society* for humanity.
Moreover, this new class society, compared to previous ones,
would likely become an *extremely strong one*.

Of course, looking back on human history,
there have been many aristocratic societies
based on slavery or serfdom, and
in Japan there was a military society (samurai society)
that made hierarchical distinctions
between samurai, farmers, artisans, and merchants.
A society falling into such categories,
which were structured based on
the *status which an individual is born into,*
may be called a *status class society*.
On the other hand, within our current capitalist society,
structured based on *owned assets* and
separated into an upper, a middle, and a lower class,
there exists what may be called an *economic class society*.

However, as the French, Russian, and other revolutions
throughout history show us,
status class societies could be transformed
if the lower classes rose up and
took power back from the government.
Also, in an **economic class society,**
an individual could climb the *social ladder*
to improve their status by accumulating assets
through effort, career choices, and success in business.

However, in the new class society created
by genetic engineering and designer baby technology,
what may be called a *biological class society*,
individuals would be categorized based on
the *physical and intellectual abilities one is born with*.
This would create a class of person
like the *invalids* of the film *Gattaca*, or
humans that have not undergone ability improvement

through genetic manipulation;
and such individuals would be unable to attain **valid** status,
even through means such as
revolution or the accumulation of assets.

To put it another way, this would be
a *society with absolutely no social mobility between classes*.
Such a society would be nothing less than a *nightmare* to
invalids born without the benefit of designer baby technology.

The Loopholes of
Top Secret Research and *Military Research*

However, there must be various counterarguments to
what I have discussed above.

One such counterargument would suggest that
designer baby technology could lead to
unforeseen negative consequences due to
the interaction of manipulated genes with other genes.
While this is a reasonable point
given the current state of things,
the field of genetic engineering is advancing rapidly,
making it quite possible that
such technical problems will be solved with time.

Another counterargument is that
designer baby technology based in genetic engineering is
currently prohibited on a global scale,
*making it unlikely that such a society will come to b*e.

Of course, it is true that, as of now,
the genetic manipulation of a fertilized human egg is forbidden
internationally due to medical risks and ethical concerns.
However, I believe it is possible that
this *principle will be broken* in the future,
in two distinct ways.

Firstly, **undemocratic states**, which can easily
hide information from their citizens and the media,
will be able to implement designer baby technology
under the guise of **top secret research**.
Secondly, the classified status of **military research**
will allow for this technology
to be implemented behind closed doors
even in **democratic states**.

The Commercialization of *Designer Baby Technology*

Furthermore,
once the implementation of
designer baby technology is achieved,
I believe it is very likely to spread quickly throughout society.

The reason for this is that
there are at all times **two aspirations** in our society.

The first is an aspiration harbored by many humans,
from the wealthy down to the poor:
to give their children
the best physical and intellectual ability possible,
no matter the cost, and by doing so,
to have them live a happier life.

The second is an aspiration held by corporations that
currently operate under *profit-chasing capitalism*:
to commodify and market, as soon as possible,
any technology that is likely to bring massive profits,
even if the technology poses certain ethical problems or
comes with a certain degree of medical risk.

By understanding such things,
it becomes possible to foresee a particular future.

70

That is, if designer baby technology is actually implemented,
and used at first for commercial purposes, it is very likely that
the state that makes this happen will be
an **undemocratic state** *that is*
at the vanguard of **profit-chasing capitalism**.

Of course, we should not allow
the development and use of such genetic engineering
to proceed without global agreement and cooperation,
but the reality is that
states conducting secret research and development do exist,
as well as a form of capitalism
which considers even medical care another way to gain profit;
and as long as such things exist in the world,
such a future is likely to come to pass.

In other words, beyond *technical problems,*
the question of whether or not
genetic engineering and designer baby technology—
technology which will greatly affect the future of humanity—
are properly developed and utilized, largely depends upon
the *maturity of global democracy and capitalism.*

What is *Happiness?*

Now that I have laid all this out, finally,
I would like to broaden this discussion
by bringing up one more extremely important issue.

Suppose that somehow this designer baby technology is
actually implemented in the future,
having solved various issues
including medical risks, problems of access for the poor,
and other social and ethical problems;
when that happens, we humans will once again
be confronted with one of our **most fundamental problems**.

That problem is this simple question: *what is happiness?*

Specifically, we will face the question of whether
this society—one in which anyone, if they so desire,
can genetically manipulate fertilized human eggs
to ensure their children have desirable abilities—
is truly a happy society.

The reason for this is that,
once designer baby technology becomes something
anyone can use, the horizon of
our *aspiration to have an exceptional child*
will expand without limit.
As a result, we will ask ourselves,
*"how much must I use genetic manipulation
before I am satisfied with my child?"*
And this question will force us to face the problem of
an *aspiration which has no end.*

This is a *fundamental problem* of humanity; namely,
"how happy is happy enough?"
In fact, as an antithesis to this question,
religious leaders and thinkers all around the world
have long preached a *classical view of happiness.*

Words of Wisdom Passed Down in Japan

That is, a view of happiness as
*accepting what the gods have given you and
living a life of gratitude.*

Now, when I think of this question of what is happiness,
I am reminded of *words of wisdom* that
have been passed down through the ages in my country Japan:

"Ware Tada Taru o Shiru"
(*I am content with what I have.*)

The development of cutting-edge science and technology
such as AI and genetic engineering
often lets the haughty thought
that *humans have become gods* creep into our minds.

However, I believe that such technological developments are
teaching us the importance of an old nostalgic set of values,
a humble way of life that encourages us to
live life with gratitude within the limits given to us.

Chapter Seven

In Which Direction Will the *Economy* Head in the Future?

—The Revival of **Altruism Economy**—

The Oldest Economic Principle of Humanity

Now, let us consider the direction in which
economy will be heading in the future.

To find the **answer** to this **question**,
we must first consider the most fundamental question:
What is economy?

This is because the majority of modern economists
tend to think of the **economy** *in a very short-sighted way*.
Specifically, most economists think of the **economy**
as a *monetary economy*.

However, when considered
from the *perspective of **cultural anthropology***
instead of *that of **economics**,*
it is clear that the **monetary economy** is not
the only economic principle in human society.

Actually, before the invention of *money* and
the birth of **monetary economy** in human history,
there existed a *barter economy* by which
people exchanged items of value amongst themselves.
Furthermore, before this **barter economy**,
there existed a *gift economy* by which
people gifted items of value to others.

This **gift economy** is a type of economy in which

people give items of value to others
as tokens of good will and affection.
In other words, this is an economy in which
people conduct economic activity
*for the purpose of **satisfaction of mind**.*
In contrast, a **monetary economy** is an economy in which
people conduct economic activity
*for the purpose of **acquisition of money**.*
Now, in modern economic terms
this **gift economy** is none other than *voluntary economy*.
In other words, the idea of **voluntary economy**
that has received attention in recent years is
the same as the **gift economy** of cultural anthropology,
which is the *oldest economic principle of humanity*.

Monetary Economy **and** *Voluntary Economy*

However,
while the ***gift economy*** is the oldest form of human economy,
this economic principle is not one that
simply disappeared with time.
In fact, *it has sustained human society throughout history*,
and is even now playing an important role
within human society in the form of the ***voluntary economy***.

For example, let us look at economic activities
such as household errands, child care, in-home education and
elderly care, community cleaning and public safety measures;
no one receives payment for such economic activities,
yet they are done out of love for
one's family, children and parents,
and furthermore out of a desire
among the local community to help one another's neighbors.

Because of this, in reality
we all go about our day-to-day lives enjoying the benefits of
this ***voluntary economy*** *(gift economy)*, and indeed,

without it the **monetary economy** *would cease to function,*
and we would become unable to maintain societal activities.
This becomes apparent when we imagine a society in which
household errands, child care, in-home education and
elderly care, community cleaning, and public safety measures
do not exist.

From the *Shadow Economy* to the *Leading Economy*

In other words, this **voluntary economy**,
in which *people perform work without pay*
for the sake of others' happiness,
may in a sense be called an ***altruism economy***.

However, this **voluntary economy (altruism economy)** has,
throughout human history,
been relegated to the position of a ***shadow economy***.
There are ***two reasons*** for this:

(1) **Voluntary economy** differs from **monetary economy**
in that *its economic activities cannot be evaluated*
by quantitative metrics such as money; and
(2) **Voluntary economy** is likely to *go unnoticed*
because its activities take place
within households and in regional corners of the world.

It is for these two reasons that,
in the field of modern economics, the voluntary economy is
not considered to be major economic activity,
and it has therefore been relegated to
the position of a ***shadow economy***.

However, this *voluntary economy*,
which is the **oldest form of human economy**
as well as an ***old nostalgic form of economy***,
is now being revived with **new value**.
In other words, the economic principle of human society

76

is undergoing *dialectic spiral development*.

What brought this about is
the *Internet revolution* that began in the 1990's.
That is to say, the Internet revolution has caused
the influence of voluntary economy
to spread rapidly all around the world.
As a result of this,
the Internet revolution has promoted voluntary economy
from a shadow economy to a leading economy.

For example, take **amazon.com**'s most highly-rated service:
book and product reviews in the form of comments.
These are written by users
who receive no payment whatsoever, and
are therefore an example of voluntary economy.
Google's search service, which is used without payment,
is also an example of voluntary economy.
Furthermore, **Linux**, a PC operating system
that was developed and continues to be improved
by thousands of programmers around the world free of charge,
is yet another example of voluntary economy.

In this way, it is because of the Internet revolution
that all around us a number of free services have been created
and voluntary economy has spread around the world.

The Birth of a *Hybrid Economy*

Now, as voluntary economy comes to carry
more and more influence,
where will the **economy** head from here on out?

In the realm of **economy**,
one more *dialectic development* will take place.
In addition to the *spiral development*
mentioned in Chapter One,

a *development based on*
the dialectic law of the interpenetration of opposites
will also occur.

That is,
new development will occur based on the law that
things which oppose and compete with each other
merge into one.

I believe, therefore, that
monetary economy *and* **voluntary economy**
will merge together and
a new economic principle that
can be called **hybrid economy** *will be created.*

To be exact, this is beyond mere *foresight*;
this hybrid economy is already becoming a *reality*, and
there are many examples around the world to support it.

Not Mere *Foresight*, but Already a *Reality*

For example, **amazon.com**, which I mentioned above,
has utilized its book and product reviews,
an example of voluntary economy,
to develop an incredibly lucrative business model.
Google has also developed
a highly profitable advertising business
around its essentially free search service.
And finally, **Linux** has been able to develop
a variety of system service businesses
related to its freely developed operating system.

In this way, business models based on
the merging of monetary economy and voluntary economy
have already been put into practice
and are thriving on the Internet in a variety of forms.

Self-serving Economy and _Altruistic Economy_

Furthermore, there are many examples of such trends
in fields besides the Internet.

For example, the **_non-profit organization (NPO)_**,
which traditionally functions
within the realm of voluntary economy,
has evolved in recent years
into the **_social entrepreneur_** or **_social business_**,
an entity that creates profit from business operations
aimed at contributing to society,
thereby making the business sustainable.

On the other hand, the **_for-profit company_**,
which traditionally functions
within the realm of monetary economy,
has evolved in recent years
into the **_social enterprise_** which places more importance on
corporate social responsibility (CSR) and
Sustainable Development Goals (SDGs).

In other words, this too is an example of
the _interpenetration of_
monetary economy _and_ **_voluntary economy._**

Now, what exactly is going on here?

Just now, I described
voluntary economy as **_altruism economy_**,
and in Chapter Four I mentioned
something called **_rational altruism_**.

This is the idea that
acting for the happiness of others brings oneself happiness.

In reality, something like this is taking place
even within the field of practical economic activities, where
*voluntary economy, that is **altruism economy**,*
is being integrated into the mainstream economy,
which is further developing monetary economy,
*or **self-serving economy**.*

Consequently,
the ***hybrid economy*** that results from such developments
can in a sense be called
a new economic principle that is
*an embodiment of **rational altruism**.*

And because of this, I believe that
this **voluntary economy** and **hybrid economy**,
which have spread around the world
since the Internet revolution,
will become a *vital economic principle* in the age to come.

Chapter Eight

In Which Direction Will *Capitalism* Head in the Future?

—The Economics of **Invisible Capital** —

Six Forms of Meta-level *Knowledge Capital*

Now, I discussed the future of **economy** in Chapter Seven
and now I would like to move on to the topic of
*where **capitalism** will be heading in the future*.

To understand this,
we must once again consider a fundamental question.
That is,
What is capital?

First, upon examining the current state of the world,
with ***monetary capitalism*** at its peak,
most economists talk about
transactions involving ***monetary capital***
as the primary form of economic activity.
However, when considering the future of capitalism,
it is rather ***knowledge capital***, and ***knowledge capitalism***
which is based upon it, that we should be thinking about.

The idea that ***knowledge*** is a significant form of capital
has been discussed for decades now by many futurists
such as Daniel Bell, Alvin Toffler, and Peter Drucker.
For this reason, the term ***knowledge capital***
should be known to all contemporary economists.
Despite this, the reality is that
no economic frameworks yet exists
*which accurately discuss **knowledge capital**.*

The biggest reason for this is that
knowledge capital is *not visible* and
cannot be calculated in the same way as *monetary capital*,
by *objective measures such as **monetary value***.

This is why, when discussing **knowledge capital,**
many economists have a common tendency
to limit their discussions to
intellectual property rights, *patents*, etc.,
which can be evaluated in terms of monetary value,
and they therefore
fail to properly evaluate the true nature of **knowledge capital**.

However, the concept of **knowledge capital** is
a broad one that originally encompasses
the following six forms of *meta-level knowledge capital*:

(1) *knowledge capital*
in the narrow sense, meaning knowledge and wisdom;
(2) *relation capital*
which facilitates the sharing of knowledge and wisdom;
(3) *trust capital*
which facilitates the building of relationships;
(4) *reputation capital*
which facilitates the creation of trust;
(5) *culture capital*
which gives value to relationships, trust, and reputation;
(6) *empathy capital*
which facilitates the creation of
relationships, trust, and reputation.

I collectively call these *six forms of capital*
invisible capital.

Business Operations Focused on *Invisible Capital*

From the first,
this **invisible capital** has played an incredibly important role
in real economic activity, business operations, etc.
This is why
truly excellent managers have always intuitively known
to prioritize **invisible capital** in their management
despite being unable to evaluate it quantitatively.

For example, the following words and phrases
have long been discussed as crucial key words in the fields of
Japanese-style management *and* ***Japanese-style capitalism***:

(1) The word "***enishi***" (*destined relationship*),
which places great importance on relationships with customers;
(2) The phrase
"It takes ten years to build trust, but a moment to lose it,"
which places importance on customers trust; and
(3) The phrase ***"Society is watching us,"***
which places importance on reputation in society.

Furthermore, let us consider *Silicon Valley*,
where capitalism thrives on a global scale.
The economy there flourishes not only due to
an abundance of venture capital and other monetary capital,
but also because the following forms of ***invisible capital***
are also common there:

(1) The sharing of ideas between people (*knowledge capital*);
(2) A wide network of human connections (*relation capital*);
(3) Public endorsements
by prominent figures and media outlets (*trust capital*);
(4) Reputation developed
by word of mouth (*reputation capital*); and
(5) A culture which sees failure in a positive light
as opportunity for learning (*culture capital*).

84

The *Two Paradigm Shifts* of Capitalism

In this way, while it has already played a crucial role
in real economic activities, business operations, etc.,
in the age to come,
this *invisible capital* will become more and more important.

The reason for this is that, as I explained in the Chapter Seven,
the influence of *voluntary economy*
will strengthen in years to come,
and the currency of such an economy is not monetary capital,
but rather *knowledge capital, relation capital, trust capital,
reputation capital, culture capital, and empathy capital—
in other words, invisible capital.*

Consequently,
if we consider the topics covered in Chapter Seven,
when discussing the *new capitalism* of the age to come,
I believe we should conceive of a capitalism
that has undergone the following *two paradigm shifts*.

(1) *A shift from a paradigm
that emphasizes **monetary economy**
to one that values **voluntary economy**,
resulting in an essentially **hybrid economy***; and
(2) *A shift from a paradigm
that emphasizes **visible capital** (monetary capital)
to one that values **invisible capital**.*

In other words, this is
a *generous capitalism that incorporates **altruism economy**,*
and a *mature capitalism that values **invisible value**.*

Methods of Evaluating *Invisible Capital*

However, when conceiving of this *new capitalism*,
we find ourselves coming up against this one **question**:
How do we evaluate invisible capital?

This is not a simple question to answer, but
I would like to share my own insights into this question
as I see things at present.

I believe it likely that what solves this problem for us
will be *artificial intelligence (AI)*.

That is because
AI has the ability to analyze vast and varied data, or *big data*,
relating to a given *evaluation object*,
in order to create a certain *evaluation metric*;
and, furthermore, AI can use *deep learning*
to develop and constantly improve its *evaluation method*.

This outstanding *quantitative evaluation ability*
possessed by AI has already been utilized
in complex games such as chess, *shogi* and *go*,
evaluating the relative advantage of two players as percentages
in real time during the game (for example, "64% vs 36%").

Consequently,
I believe that in the near future we will find a way to use
AI's excellent **ability to perform quantitative evaluations** of
the knowledge, relation, trust, reputation, and culture capital,
or *invisible capital*,
held by states, regions, and corporations.

Furthermore,
through our use of AI abilities,
I believe what we can accomplish will not stop
at the evaluation of **invisible capital**,

but will expand to the evaluation of *social prosperity*
through the calculation of indicators.

Specifically, I mean the calculation of indicators like
Gross Domestic Well-being (GDW) and
Gross National Happiness (GNH).

These indicators are different from
Gross Domestic Product (GDP)
which can be measured by a single monetary term;
rather, GDW and GNH are by nature
made up of various elements
which must be evaluated comprehensively,
making quantitative evaluation difficult.
In the near future, however,
I believe that through the use of AI and big data,
we will create effective metrics
for the evaluation of such indicators.

Future Generations as *Stakeholders*

The above is my personal insight into the *future of capitalism*,
but I would also like to discuss a new type of capitalism
that was recently proposed at the **World Economic Forum,**
the parent organization to the Global Agenda Council
I used to be a member of.
The new form of capitalism proposed
by the World Economic Forum is *stakeholder capitalism*.

This would be a more mature form of capitalism
than the traditional *shareholder capitalism*
which only focuses on the profits of **shareholders**.
But if we truly wish to pursue this **stakeholder capitalism**,
there is *one group of people*
we must include under the category of stakeholder.

That is, *future generations*.

Among Native Americans
there are some **words of wisdom** that come to mind:
The earth, we are borrowing it from our descendants.

If we look at the **imbalance** of modern capitalism which
expends resources and destroys the global environment
without limit,
it is clear to anyone that
a *new form of capitalism which deeply considers*
*the benefit of **future generations*** must be created.

The Meaning of *Rational Altruism* We Can Learn from AI

Now, as ***future generations*** do not yet exist,
who would be able to stand in their place and
advocate for their rights and opinions?

It is of course very important that
people who are *sympathetic* to **future generations**
and who have great *scientific knowledge and imagination*
to foresee the future,
speak in the stead of those who cannot speak for themselves.

However, this problem, too, may be solved by *AI*;
through the use of big data and vast scientific knowledge,
AI will be able to run countless future simulations
in order to *represent and speak up*
*for the interests of **future generations***.

I say this because I believe
AI would not be affected by small concerns of
individual interests or positions,
nor that they would be swayed by emotion.
AI would merely take into account
*the interests of **future generations***
when making decisions and recommendations.

88

The decisions and recommendations of such AI
could in a sense teach us, who are
so stained by the selfish values of **gluttonous capitalism**,
about the *true meaning of **rational altruism**.*

And finally,
if humanity in the future creates a ***world government***
to represent the interests of all people in the world,
the incredible abilities of AI
that ***can make judgements fairly and without ego,***
from a scientific and objective perspective,
will no doubt become
a vital part of this government's faculties.

Chapter Nine

In Which Direction Will *Democracy* Head in the Future?

—Toward a True **Participatory Democracy** —

The Spiral Development
That Will Also Occur in *Democracy*

Now, *in what direction will **democracy** head in the future*?

In Chapter Seven, I explained that
a dialectic *spiral development* is taking place
with regards to the **economic principle** of human society.
Now, I also believe that a similar spiral development will occur
with regards to **democracy** in the future.

That is, in the age to come,
I believe that **direct democracy**, which was
human society's primary form of democracy in the past,
will be revived in a new form.

If we look back upon human history,
we can see that **direct democracy** was common in the past;
in the small primitive communities of the past,
community policies would be decided on
by gathering together members of the community.

Furthermore, this primitive form of **direct democracy** existed
as a precise method of state management
in ancient Greece and the Roman Republic.

However, as human civilization developed,
the population of communities, societies, and states grew,
making **direct democracy** difficult to maintain

as it lost its former *efficiency and speed.*
As time passed,
direct democracy was replaced by **indirect democracy**,
which has become the main form of democracy
in modern times.
This is both the **presidential system**
by which citizens cast votes to nominate a national leader,
and the **parliamentary system**
by which citizens cast votes to nominate representatives.

The Various Problems Facing *Indirect Democracy*

However, in recent years
many problems have been pointed out
with regards to the **presidential** and **parliamentary systems**.

One such problem is that,
despite the fact that
the public opinion of citizens changes rapidly,
accompanied by the rapid change of circumstances
surrounding society and the state,
the public opinion is only reflected in government
once every few years when an election is held.

Another problem is that
the ***single-member district system*** sometimes results in
a political party with 30 percent or less of the vote
gaining over 60 percent of the seats in government,
a situation that *cannot be said to*
accurately reflect the opinions of citizens.
On the other hand,
while the ***multi-member district system***
more accurately reflects the opinions of citizens,
it also results in a proliferation of many small political parties,
which make *coming to a consensus* and
deciding on consistent policies *difficult.*
In this way, modern society,

which is based on **indirect democracy**,
is facing the very difficult problems mentioned above.
With that in mind, what is going to happen going forward?

Interpenetration to Occur in the *Two Democracies*

I believe that ***direct democracy***,
which seems to have disappeared from society,
will be revived in a new form.
Furthermore, *this **direct democracy** will merge with*
***indirect democracy** to create a new form of democracy.*

It is apparent that
both *the Internet revolution and the information revolution*
will make this possible.
Thanks to these two revolutions,
nearly all people in developed countries are able to
use their *smartphones and computers*
to *freely express their opinions*
on *social media and other web-based platforms*.

Furthermore,
using social media and other web-based platforms,
mass media has also *improved*
its ability to easily hear the opinions of the masses
by conducting large-scale public surveys,
which can be done in a short time and at no significant cost.

Under such circumstances,
public opinion, which is frequently changing,
can have influence over mass media
through social media and other web-based platforms;
this has created a situation in which,
even in a society governed by indirect democratic systems
such as the **presidential** and **parliamentary systems**,
public opinion can affect
government policies relatively quickly.

This means that
a ***direct democracy culture*** *is spreading throughout society*
due to the Internet and information revolutions,
and it is in the *process of*
merging with the ***indirect democracy system***.

<u>Serious Problem of *Populism*</u>

However, the revival of a culture of direct democracy
does not mean that
only the positive elements of that culture will be realized.
There are some big problems that will occur
because of this revival.

One of these problems is that of ***populism***
which is symbolized by the Trump era of the US.
In other words, this is the trend toward a politics that
only touts short-term policies which appeal to the masses,
paying no heed to
the big picture or the long-term benefits of citizens,
and a ***rabble-rousing politics***
born as a result of the direct connection
between political leaders and the people, the media, etc.,
which social media has made possible.

If so, in an age when
the Internet and information revolutions are strengthening
trends toward a direct democratic political culture,
what should we do
to realize a healthy and mature form of democracy
that is not distorted by rabble-rousing politics or populism?

The *Mirror* Reflecting the Mind of the People

We should recall this important warning
often touted in the field of political science:
The government of a single state is
an **unclouded mirror** *reflecting the mind of the people.*

In other words,
to realize a mature form of democracy within our state,
the *very consciousness of each of us as citizens, one by one*,
must ultimately *mature*.
There is no other way than this.
No matter how much we reform our political system
or introduce new political systems,
we will never be able to realize a mature form of democracy
as long as the citizens' consciousness remains
so near-sighted, materialistic, and self-centered.

If so, what is necessary to
the maturing of the consciousness of citizens
toward their government?

To effect this maturing, it is of course extremely important
to conduct a thorough **democracy education**,
starting from childhood education and
continuing into adulthood education.

Considering even the single issue of the global environment,
without appropriate democracy education,
there is no way for citizens to develop a mature consciousness
and to express their opinions to the government,
taking into consideration things on a global level,
as well as the well-being of future generations.

94

The True Meaning of the Word *"Participation"*

However, there is one perspective that is often lost
in democracy education.

That is, the question of
what participation is in a **democracy**.
For example, when we talk about the limits and problems of
our current indirect democracy, or *representative democracy*,
we must stress the importance of realizing direct democracy,
or *participatory democracy*, to replace it.

However, for us to do this,
it is necessary to understand
the *true meaning of* **participation**
in a *participatory democracy*.

That is because we often make the mistake of thinking that
participation in a participatory democracy means
simply *participation in* **society's decision-making**.
That is, we think that
participating in elections and the national vote to determine
various *government policies*,
various *political parties*, and
various *political candidates*,
is *participation*.

However, this is not true.
Participation in a direct democracy actually means
participation in **social transformation**.

If we simply think that participatory democracy means
participating in **society's decision-making**,
then we get swept away in the idea that
the *execution of the decisions made* should be ultimately
left in the hands of politicians and bureaucracy.

The Words of Dramatist Bertolt Brecht

There is a famous speech which sounded
the warning bell of this danger of public awareness.
That speech is
the historic inaugural address of **John F. Kennedy** in 1961.

"Ask not what your country can do for you.
Ask what you can do for your country."

This historic speech written by Theodore C. Sorensen sounded
the alarm against the dangers of **populism**
as a perversion of democracy created
by a citizens' consciousness that
only thinks about *what the government can do for me*.
And furthermore, it stressed the *importance of participation*
through the efforts of each citizen
to build a better society and a better state.

From all this we see that
true democracy is a democracy based on
the fundamental premise that
each of us participates in social transformation,
and that, without a citizenry made up of individuals
with a strong, *independent consciousness*,
we will undoubtedly fall into a *dependent consciousness* that
believes that *someone else will change this state for me*.
Such a consciousness is fertile ground for
hero-waiting and *populism* to sprout up from.

As another famous saying
regarding the *dangers of a dependent consciousness*
harbored by citizens,
I would like to share
the words of German dramatist **Bertolt Brecht**,
from his play **"Life of Galileo"**:

"Unhappy is not the land that breeds no hero.
Unhappy is the land that needs a hero."

These are words that we should consider deeply
when thinking about or discussing **democracy**.

Changemakers **Called** *Social Entrepreneurs*

Now, what exactly does it mean that
each of us participates in **societal transformation**?

To teach us the answer to this question,
I offer the words of Bill Drayton, representative of Ashoka,
a non-profit organization that supports a great number of
social entrepreneurs active all around the world:

"Everyone a changemaker."

In other words, Bill Drayton is saying that
anyone can change society
through the work they do every day,
and *social entrepreneurs*, who begin enterprises and
do business with the express purpose of
social contribution and social transformation,
are a symbol of this very idea.

Furthermore, this is not limited to social entrepreneurs,
but rather anyone can, through their day-to-day work,
contribute to and change society for the better.

This is because,
no matter how modest your work, it is part of
what supports our society and has significance in it.
So, *by working harder to do a better job every day,*
we are working toward creating a better society.

The *Spirit of Societal Contribution* of the Japanese View of Work

Such an idea has been passed down
as a ***clear cultural concept*** in *Japan*.
That is because it is said that
the *Japanese word for "work,"* **hataraku,** *is*
the act of "making your neighbor happy"
(**hata** means **"neighbor"** and **raku** means **"happiness"**).

In other words, in Japan
there exists an excellent ***view of work*** which defines work
as ***doing something for our neighbors' happiness***
based on the *premise of social contribution*;
therefore, there also exists a unique culture of work
which emphasizes the ***joy of work***
by which we derive joy from our day-to-day work
being useful in the world.

To put it another way,
work *is something like* ***altruism*** in Japan,
and our ***view of work*** *is one which includes*
a sense of ***social contribution.***

Of course, in Japan it is not always the case that
all workers can have this sort of consciousness.

In reality, there are many types of work
which do not give workers a sense of the joy of work, and
there are also many people who feel their work is **drudgery**.
Furthermore, there are many workplaces where
a majority of the work being done is this kind of work.

However, as I explained in Chapter Five,
the *robotics revolution and the AI revolution will create*
the foundation for many people to be able to engage in
sophisticated work which offers greater joy.

This means that, at the same time as such revolutions,
we will be able to make way for
a *new age in which everyone can have a sense that
they are contributing to and transforming society
through their work.*

I believe that when we make way for such an age,
we will finally be able to realize
a *true* **participatory democracy**.

Chapter Ten

In Which Direction Will *Religion* Head in the Future?

— The Merging of **Religion** and **Science** —

<u>The Interpenetration of *Religion* and *Science*</u>

Now, *in what direction will **religion** head in the future?*

With regard to this theme,
I would again like to try foreseeing the future
using one of the *laws of dialectic development*.

That law is the ***law of interpenetration of opposites***.

This is, as I have explained previously,
the law which states that
things which oppose and compete with one another
come to incorporate each other's essential characteristics
and merge with one another.

According to this law, I believe
*in the future **religion** and **science** will merge.*

Looking back on history, we see from examples
such as the 17th-century **trial of Galileo**,
that there was an age
in which religion considered science ***its enemy***,
and even suppressed science because of this.
However,
most people in modern times study science in school education,
believe scientific recognition to be correct, and
benefit from science in the form of technology every day.

Therefore,
if we call **religion** that which people **believe** in,
it is apparent that
the greatest religion of modern times is **science**.

Now, amidst such social circumstances,
many religions in modern times have come to
incorporate scientific knowledge.

In other words, there has been a *tendency for religions*
to incorporate the **rationalism** *of science.*
However, the opposite tendency has also come about
in modern times: that is,
science has taken steps toward the **spiritualism** *of religion.*

Modern Science Moving towards *Mysticism*

In reality, you can see the *colors of a deep spiritualism*
in the most cutting-edge theories of modern science.

For example, regarding the origin of the world,
Christianity holds that, according to
the Book of Genesis in the Old Testament of the Bible,
"God created the world in seven days."

On the other hand, the **Inflation Cosmology**,
which is one of modern science's cutting-edge theories,
explains the origin of the universe with a story
that goes like this:

13.8 billion years ago, the universe did not exist.
Instead, there existed an extremely small **quantum vacuum**.
However, in a moment,
a **fluctuation** occurred within this quantum vacuum, and
in the next moment a sudden **Inflation** took place.
The next moment, the **Big Bang** occurred, and
this universe began to expand at the speed of light.

As a result of this, 13.8 billion years later in the present day,
this universe has expanded to
a vastness of 13.8 billion light years, and
contains roughly 200 billion galaxies,
each of which contains roughly 200 billion stars.

Hearing this story of **genesis**, or
the birth of the universe *as told by cutting-edge science*,
we are filled with an even greater *sense of mysticism*
than Christianity's Book of Genesis gives us.

And yet, it is fascinating to see the strange similarities
between these two stories of genesis.

The Strange Similarities
between *Classical Religion* and *Modern Science*

That is, according to cutting-edge cosmology,
immediately after the birth of the universe
due to the Inflation and the Big Bang,
this universe was flooded with photons.
In other words, it was *filled with light.*

On the other hand,
the Book of Genesis in the Old Testament of the Bible
begins like this:

God said,
"Let there be light."
And there was light.

Is this similarity between the two stories above
a mere coincidence?

But the strange similarities between religion and science
do not end there.

Modern cosmology says that
this vast universe was born from a **quantum vacuum**,
but actually, the **Heart Sutra**,
an important sacred text in Buddhism, also states that
"Form itself is emptiness.
Emptiness itself is form."
(Shiki-soku-ze-ku, Ku-soku-ze-shiki).

Is this also mere coincidence?

It is fascinating to examine these strange similarities between
the stories of classical religion and those of modern science.
But in any case,
such stories of genesis, told by modern science,
fill us with a *mysterious sense of mysticism*.

However,
this **Inflation Cosmology** has yet another theoretical concept
which gives us an even more mysterious sense of mysticism.

Cosmological Darwinism **and the** *Miracle Universe*

That is, the theoretical concept of
Cosmological Darwinism.

According to this theory,
the fluctuation of a quantum vacuum
gives birth to infinite *baby universes*,
each of which have their own unique
combination of natural physical constants.
(A natural physical constant dictates the numerical values of
gravity, electromagnetism, and mass of neutrons and protons.)

The theory goes on to state that
only the universe that by chance has
the most optimal combination of natural physical constants
can continue to exist.

According to this theory, for example,
a difference as small as *one in a trillion* to
the initial speed of a universe's expansion may have caused
such baby universes to *disperse or to collapse*,
and therefore to cease to exist.

In other words,
according to this theory of **Cosmological Darwinism**,
this universe we live in, which was
one of an overwhelmingly vast number of **baby universes**,
miraculously survived against astounding odds;
truly, there is no more fitting description for this universe than
to call it a **miracle universe**.

And if this is true,
when we look up at the stars in the night sky,
we will naturally be enveloped in a *deep sense of gratitude*.
We should feel gratitude for
the *miracle of our **very existence***.

The Mystery of *Parallel Universe Cosmology*

Furthermore, there is a recent theory
in cutting-edge cosmology that gives us
an unimaginable sense of mysticism
beyond that of **Cosmological Darwinism**.
That is, the theory of ***Parallel Universe Cosmology***.

This theory claims that there are universes other than ours
which *miraculously survived*
after they were created by
the fluctuation of the quantum vacuum, and
they have formed *parallel worlds*.
Because of this, leading authorities in cosmology
call this collection of parallel universes
not a ***uni-verse***, but rather a ***multi-verse***.

In this way, the **genesis** of the world according to
modern science's cutting-edge cosmological theories
gives humans a **deep sense of mysticism**
even greater than that of the myths told by classical religion.

Our Worldview Changed by
the *Theory of Relativity* and *Quantum Physics*

However, it is not only modern cosmology that
gives us such a sense of mysticism.

At the time,
the *theory of relativity* advocated by Albert Einstein,
which claimed that the progression of time
can change depending on location
and that gravity can influence the progression of time,
flipped what people held as common sense on its head.

Furthermore,
quantum physics advocated by Werner Heisenberg and others
holds that all matter simultaneously has
two mutually contradictory natures;
that is, all matter behaves both as a wave and a particle.
This theory once again teaches us a reality which
our daily experience would not enable us to fully understand.

Stated like this, we find that
the worldview shown to humans
by cutting-edge theories of modern science are
filled with a deep spirituality even greater than
that of the myths, legends, and allegories
told to humans by classical religions.
Therefore, those who hear these stories of modern science are
filled with a deeply profound sense of wonder and awe.

An Age when *Religion* and *Science* Will Merge

And if the origin of **religion** is in
this *sense of wonder* toward the world,
then there is no doubt that
it is cutting-edge modern science that
gives us the most utterly profound **sense of wonder**.

In this way, at the present day,
religion is taking on
the **rationalism** *and* **logicality** *of science*
while science is stepping into
the realm of religion's **spiritualism** *and* **sense of wonder**.
In a sense, this represents the coming of an age in which
religion and **science** will interpenetrate and merge together.

If this is true,
what we should now talk about when discussing **religion** is
neither **criticism** nor **advocacy** of classical religion.

Rather, we should consider the vision of the future
I have discussed in my book ***Death Does Not Exist***—
a future in which *religion and science will merge together*.

106

Chapter Eleven

In Which Direction Will *Art* Head in the Future?

— Human Life as **Art** —

<u>The Vision of Karl Marx and Kenji Miyazawa</u>

In Chapter Ten, I talked about the future of **religion**.
Now, my next question is,
*in which direction will **art** head in the future?*

In the past,
the economist **Karl Marx** (author of the historic work ***Capital***)
foresaw that capitalism would develop to
a certain level of sophistication,
after which a new wealthy society of the future would emerge;
and within that society, advanced technologies would spread
and society's productivity would skyrocket,
liberating humans from the shackles of hard labor
and giving them a *great deal of free time.*

He further foresaw that, in this future society,
many people would use their newfound free time to engage in
the *creation of painting, music, poetry and literature—*
in other words, they would begin to engage in ***artistic activity.***

Similarly,
the Japanese folk poet **Kenji Miyazawa** has expressed
his vision of a future society in the following words:
*"The day will come, when a hundred million artists, and
a hundred million poets are born, one day."*

Now, if we look at reality,
we see that, as the ***Fourth Industrial Revolution*** proceeds,

primarily in developed countries,
robotics, artificial intelligence (AI), Internet,
virtual reality (VR), drone and
self-driving automobile technologies are spreading,
and many people are being liberated,
first from *simple manual labor*,
and then from *routine knowledge work* as well.
Of course, the *time people must work* is
also becoming shorter.

As a result of all this,
as Karl Marx foresaw and Kenji Miyazawa dreamed,
many people will come to enjoy a surplus of free time,
and using that time, they will engage in
various creative and artistic activities from here on out.

With this in mind, in this Chapter Eleven
I would like to focus on
discussing **two problems** regarding the future of **art**.

The *Advance of Science* and the *Evolution of Art*

The first problem is,
from here on out, how will art evolve?

From the start,
that which we call **art** comes in many forms and genres,
and its evolution can also take on a variety of forms,
making it difficult to discuss them all in simple terms.

Therefore, if I can express one of my questions at present
concerning the *evolution of art*, the question of
*"how will the development of cutting-edge technologies
influence the evolution of art?"*
would become a deeply intriguing topic.

Firstly, the development of *robotics* will

not only free humans from manual labor;
but it also has the potential to bring about
innovation in the art world.

For example, I believe the abilities of robots
will be utilized to create paintings and sculptures
according to the creative vision of a human artist
and a new style of painting and sculpting will be born
from *cooperative work between robots and humans*.

In the 2004 American sci-fi movie *i, Robot*,
there is a scene in which the robot Sunny
skillfully sketches out a picture using both hands,
but in reality this sort of thing is already possible.

Also, the development of *AI* will
not only free humans from routine knowledge work,
but it will also give rise to a new style of art.

It is technically possible to use AI
to create music, pictures, or videos
based on the novel ideas of humans.
Actually, a human can instruct an AI to make
a musical piece in the style of Brian Eno's ambient music,
and the AI will instantly compose a piece
according to this instruction.

Furthermore, advances in cutting-edge technology
have made possible artistic expression
that was previously impossible to achieve.

For example,
artists are able to paint digital pictures of three dimensions
within a virtual three-dimensional space,
which people can enjoy by entering this virtual space
wearing VR goggles.
Such art is already a reality.

And where such art is possible,
it also becomes easy for people to
participate in such a three-dimensional painting.
As a result,
the **artist and audience** dichotomy
that has defined art up until now
will evolve into a new mode of art
that may be called *viewer participatory painting* or
collaborative painting between painter and participant.

This is not limited
just to painting, graphics, and other *visual arts,*
but can be applied
to music, acoustics, and other forms of *sound art.*
These will surely evolve into
listener participatory music or
collaborative music between musician and participant.

This evolution toward *participatory art* is incredibly difficult
to achieve through traditional means such as
paint on canvas, live music using actual instruments, etc.
What has made this evolution toward participatory art possible
are digital and VR technologies
which enable *any number of participants*
to freely create their **own work of art.**

The Age in Which *Work* Will be Regarded as *Art*

Now, the above paragraphs cover
my vision of the first problem:
From here on out, how will art evolve?

The second problem is,
from here on out,
what sorts of things will deepen to the level of art?

Regarding this problem, my vision is that,

*in the coming age **work** will undergo a deepening*
*so that it can be called **art**.*

Before, I stated my foresight that
the time people spend on work will shorten, and
the time people engage in art will grow,
but actually, I believe that
there will be one other development,
in a dialectic sense, that will occur at the same time.

That is,
*that **work** will no longer be considered the opposite of **art**,*
*but rather it will become a form of **art** itself.*

In other words,
work *will become a form of artistic activity*
*involving the making of creative **works of art**.*

Of course, this development will not occur
in every form of work in modern society,
but it will spread throughout fields
in which *advanced skills and abilities* are required.

In reality, even before now, in various fields
top-class professionals have exhibited
extremely sophisticated techniques and creativity
which have allowed them to be elevated in some way
into the artistic realm.

One such example is the *culinary chef.*
For chefs at first rate restaurants,
the cuisine they provide to customers is not mere ***product***,
but a ***work of art*** of their creativity.
Because of this,
customers come to the restaurant to taste and enjoy
this cuisine which is a **creative work**.

Furthermore, this phenomenon is not limited to

112

high-end restaurants that cater to the rich.
For example, in Japan
there are many **corner stores** catering to ordinary people
that serve *ramen*, a common dish enjoyed by the masses.
More than a few of the owners of such ramen shops
take their work seriously enough to be elevated to
the realm of the artistic.

In fact, the most popular ramen shops in big cities
have long lines of customers waiting every day, and
shop owners carefully make their noodles,
soup and other ingredients
to offer unique, creative ramen dishes, and yet
they maintain a low price that is affordable to ordinary people.
The owners of such shops are a kind of artist,
and they believe that their ramen is
a *creative work that only they can offer*.

Now, the *elevation of* **work** *to* **artistic activity**
is certainly not limited to the culinary world.
First-rate *hotel employees* in Europe and America,
for example, consider their customer services
to be a kind of intangible art, and
they therefore go about their day-to-day work with pride.
Furthermore, in Japan, as indicated by the popular phrases
omotenashi (hospitality) and
ichigo-ichie (a once-in-a-lifetime encounter),
customer service is not simply a service,
but a very unique personal undertaking,
a one-time artistic undertaking, and even
a *deeply religious undertaking* with spiritual significance.

Individuality and *Once-ness*

In this way, we can see this
undertaking of elevating **work** *to a kind of* **artistic activity**

not only in the culinary and customer service fields,
but also in various fields
requiring sophisticated skills and creativity,
and in the background of such undertakings
there are two profound ideas.

One idea is *individuality*.

In other words,
there is the idea of **individuality** in the form of
something that only a certain individual can provide, or
something that only a certain individual can create.
This idea exists in the background of **artistry**.

The other idea is *once-ness*.

Earlier, I explained the Japanese idea of
ichigo-ichie (a once-in-a-lifetime encounter)
in relation to *omotenashi* (hospitality).
Now, in the *transformation of interpersonal work*,
such as customer service, management, education,
and consulting, into a kind of *artistic activity*,
the idea of **once-ness** comes to play an important role
in the sense that *as a result of the meeting of two people
at a certain place and at a certain moment,
a unique, one-time occurrence happens*.

Human Life as Supreme Art

However, as we discuss the *true nature of art* in this way,
we come to realize one deep truth.

If the true nature of **art** is *individuality* in the sense of
something which only a specific person can create,
as well as *once-ness* in the sense of a one-time occurrence,
then *our life also becomes none other than art itself*.

114

The reason for this is that
each of our lives is a *one-time* thing no matter who we are, and
each represents the undertaking of carving out
an ***individual road*** only one person can walk, and
doing one's best to ***express who one is*** on that road
amid the various ***constraints and adversities***
presented to that person.

And that is undoubtedly a kind of **art**.
It is in fact none other than the ***greatest art*** that
we humans can undertake.

However, if our **life** is the **greatest art**,
then it is set against the backdrop of the undeniable facts that
*our life is a **one-time thing**, and that its **end** is sure to come.*

In other words,
at its foundation exists the *reality of **death***.

Death surely comes to everyone.
But it is precisely because there is an ***end of life*** that
our lives become the **greatest art**.

However, if that is the truth, then we must confront
the **most important question** that has faced humanity
since the beginning of human history.

That is the question:
what is death?

And furthermore,
*if **death** did not exist,*
*what would our **life** then become?*

This is a question we must face.

In the final chapter of this section, Chapter Twelve,
I would like to discuss this topic further.

Will *Immortality* Become a Reality in the Future?

— The Ultimate Unhappiness Called **Immortality** —

Immortality from Science Fantasy to Realistic Science

In Chapter Eleven, I stated that
death surely comes to human life.

In the sense of the **death of the physical body**,
this is an undeniable truth that anyone today will acknowledge,
but in the not-so-distant future
the day will come when this **truth** is flipped on its head.

I ask this question because,
amidst the rapid advancements of
cutting-edge science and modern medicine,
the possibility of *realizing* **human immortality** is
being seriously discussed.

First of all,
advancements in *biotechnology and nanotechnology* are
increasing the likelihood of conquering diseases
which have up until now been considered
uncurable illnesses such as cancer.

Furthermore,
advancements in *cloning and organ transplantation* have
opened the possibility of indefinitely extending human life
through the continual transplantation of healthy organs
to replace ones that have become sick,
which would be possible
so long as the human's brain remains healthy.

In addition,
the developments made in the fields of
artificial organ creation and robotics
will even enable us to compensate for physical disabilities
through man-made technologies.

Also, as the futurist **Ray Kurzweil** explains
in his book ***The Singularity Is Near***,
the day will come when we are able to copy and transfer
the contents of the *human brain* itself onto a computer, and
Kurzweil predicts that this will happen in the early 2040s.

I myself am skeptical of Kerzweil's prediction that
the contents of a human brain
can be transplanted into a computer,
but it was the sci-fi film ***Transcendence***, starring Johnny Depp,
which imagined such technology as a reality.

In this way, the rapid advancements
in cutting-edge technology and modern medicine are
changing our discussion of human **immortality**
from one of ***theoretical scientific imagination***
to one of ***real scientific possibility***.

The *Unhappiness* Brought about by *Immortality*

However, what I want to discuss here is
not the technical possibility of making **immortality** a reality
using science and technology
which humans will develop in the future,
but rather, *whether **immortality** will truly*
*bring **happiness** to humanity.*

To state my conclusion first, I believe that,
even if science and medical advancements of the future
*really do make human **immortality** possible,*
*rather than **happiness** it will bring us **unhappiness**.*

The reason for this is that,
no matter how advanced our **immortality** technology becomes,
there will still be *those who cannot benefit from it,*
and who nonetheless must face **death**.

They will be people who find themselves
in the following *two circumstances*.

The *Economically Destitute*

First are *those who are poor and*
therefore unable to access **immortality technology**.

The *sense of unfairness* which
such people will feel toward the rich
will be one of utter desperation far greater than that
brought about by economic disparity up until now.
That is because the old saying that
death is doled out to everyone equally
will no longer be true.
For this reason,
the feelings of those who cannot obtain **immortality**
towards those who can,
will at times become something close to *resentment or fury*.

For example, the 2011 American sci-fi movie *In Time*,
directed by **Andrew Niccol**, symbolically depicts
the tragedy of such a world in which
while the rich can buy unending life,
the poor must live short lives.

Those Who Suffer *Destructive Accidents*

Second are *people* who *die*
due to their body being physically destroyed.

118

In other words, no matter how advanced
our medical treatments and regenerative technologies become,
there will still be no treatment or method of recovery
if the body is completely destroyed or disintegrated
in destructive events such as car accidents and fires.

Now, this reality is in a way quite common-sensical, but
it will *have an extremely profound effect on our psychology.*

This is because we will have no choice
but to **live an extremely cowardly life**
in the face of this reality.

In other words, under circumstances in which
we can have **extremely long life** or even **eternal life**
as long as we avoid tragic accidents in which
the body may be completely destroyed or disintegrated,
we will become obsessively concerned with avoiding
any actions which present the danger of such an accident.

For example, as of now, most of us
are able to ride in an *airplane* with little sense of fear,
even though there is a small chance of a plane crash.

In the back of our minds,
we think to ourselves something like the following:

"Statistically, airplane accidents are very rare,
so it is unlikely the plane will crash.
I would have to be extremely unlucky
to be on a plane that crashes.
And anyway, *all humans die eventually.*"

In other words, we have
a mentality which unconsciously accepts death.

However, in a society in which
it is possible to have **extremely long life** or **eternal life**

as long as we live our lives carefully,
even a ride in an airplane will become frightening.
Though the chances are very low,
if the plane does crash
one's body may be completely destroyed, and therefore
the possibility of **immortality** will be completely lost.

In other words,
it will become unacceptable to risk danger
*when considering the **magnitude of what could be lost**.*

Because of this, people will come to avoid
dangerous sports such as rock climbing and sky diving.
This is because people only engage in
such sports that *flirt with death*
because in their hearts they believe that
everyone dies eventually,
so I want to make this moment shine
and live a fulfilling life.

Those Who Lose *Loved Ones*

Furthermore, in such a society
in which *medical immortality is realized*,
the *loss of a loved one* to a destructive accident
will bring about a *sense of despair* far deeper than
what we have experienced up until now.

This is because when loved ones die now,
we are comforted by the *understanding and resignation* that
everyone dies eventually, and sooner or later
we must part in death with our loved ones,
and the *religious expectation* that
I too will die eventually, and when I do,
I will be able to meet with my loved ones again
in the afterlife.

120

In **Ridley Scott**'s famous movie *Gladiator*,
protagonist Maximus' slave friend says the following words
after Maximus' death:
"See you again. But not now."

These words,
which express the *idea that we may meet again after death*,
represent a *thought for peace of mind* in a world
in which **death** is unavoidable.

However, in a world in which **immortality** is realized,
the thought of **meeting again after death**
will no longer help us.
Upon losing a loved one,
we will fall into *hopelessness*, thinking
"why did you alone die and lose your eternal life?"

In this way, even if **immortality** becomes medically possible,
we will be forced to confront the problem of
whether humans at that time will truly be happy.

To me, this will rather bring
ultimate unhappiness to humanity.

What We Will Lose with *Endless Life*

Now, up until now I have discussed the problems given
circumstances in which there are people
*who cannot enjoy the benefits of **immortality**.*
However, even if *we are able to*
*completely realize **immortality** for all people*,
there is one more problem we will then face.

That is,
*when we have attained **eternal life**,*
*we will no longer feel that **time** has any value and*

will therefore lose our mind to use the time before us
as something important and meaningful
to live a fulfilling life from day to day.

In other words,
it is precisely because the time span of our lives is limited
that we consider life to be irreplaceable
and use the time given to us well,
praying that we live our lives in a fulfilling way
from day to day.

Keeping in mind the fact
that our lives each come to an end eventually,
we wish to do something good,
to leave behind something wonderful in the world
as proof that we lived, even after we are gone;
we set *goals and make plans*, harbor *dreams and ideals*, and
do our utmost while we live to make these things a reality.

Furthermore, these wishes we each harbor and
ways of living we each attempt are
what contribute to the *advancement of humanity as a whole*;
and the reason we have children whom we raise with love and
entrust the future to with our earnest prayers,
is that we hope that we may leave our dreams and ideals
for the next generation to continue after we are gone.

It is the passing on of such dreams and ideals
that has for thousands of years helped advance humanity.

Physicist **Freeman Dyson** once stated in an interview that
death is the greatest invention;
because of it,
we are able to yield our place to younger generations,
and humanity is able to advance.

I believe these are extremely profound words.

That Which Shines Because of *Death*

If we understand life as I have discussed it in this final chapter,
we finally come to realize a certain *paradox* of human life:

*Because there is **death**,*
***human life** shines.*

This is the **great paradox** of human life.
Moreover, if we understand this paradox,
then I believe we must walk through life
always keeping our eyes on the following *three truths*,
in order to make our **irreplaceable lives** shine bright:

Our life will surely come to an end.
Our life occurs only once.
No one knows when the end will come.

It is because of these truths that
we can have gratitude towards the life we are given,
cherish every irreplaceable moment of that life,
live each day to the fullest, and
feel profound joy in meeting other people in our lives.

Part II

The *Five Laws* to Foresee the Future

The **Next Changes**
Foreseen by Dialectic Thinking

The Key to Foreseeing the Future Lies in *Dialectic Thinking*.

The **Five Laws** of Dialectic.

We *cannot predict* the future.

But

we can *foresee* it.

We want to know the future.

Everyone harbors such a thought.

If we could predict the future,
an individual could open up their own life.
Businesspersons and executives
could develop their businesses or companies
while politicians and administrators
could bring prosperity to the state and society.

If it were really possible to predict the future,
we could solve many problems facing us.

Everyone harbors such thoughts, such desires.
For that very reason, the world is flooded with
all kinds of books on *predicting the future*.

But in the coming age,
we must admit one fact.

We cannot predict the future.

That is an undeniable fact.
And there are three reasons for it.

*The first is **discontinuity**.*

Most of the changes that will occur in the coming age
will not be **continuous** changes.
***Discontinuous** and **dramatic** changes,*
cut off from the past, will occur.
So the word *evolution* is often used in the world.
In such an age, *we cannot predict the future*
by extrapolating from the changes of the past.
Just by investigating and analyzing ***past tendencies**,*
we cannot see the future.
The future will come suddenly cut off from the past.
This is the first reason.

*The second is **non-linearity**.*

In addition to **discontinuity**,
this **non-linearity** makes prediction even harder.
*Even a **slight fluctuation** in a corner of society*
*can cause an **enormous change** of society as a whole.*
The metaphor often used for this is
the ***butterfly effect**.*

The three reasons

we *cannot predict* the future:

discontinuity, *non-linearity*, *acceleration*.

When a butterfly flutters its wings in Beijing,
a hurricane occurs in New York.
This is the so-called **non-linear** effect.
In other words, *a slight fluctuation* at present
can cause **enormous changes** in the future.
So if we just look at *current major trends*,
we cannot know the future.
This is the second reason.

The third is **acceleration**.

This is the age of the *dog year* in which
changes that took 7 years in the past
occur in one year in the present.
And now we have the *mouse year* in which
changes that took 18 years in the past
occur in one year.
Changes of all things have been accelerated.
And in such an age,
when we predict the future,
the future has already gone by.

130

Therefore,
if we think only of *changes in the near future*,
we actually cannot see the future itself.
This is the third reason.

That is,
discontinuity,
non-linearity,
acceleration.

These three factors, in the present time,
make **predicting the future** extremely difficult.

Now then, what should we do?

If we **cannot predict** the future, what should we do?

Answering this question is the purpose of this Part II.
So right here in the beginning,
I will present the answer.

*We **cannot predict** the future.*
*But we **can foresee** it.*

That is the answer.
If so, what do these words mean?

We cannot predict *specific changes*.

However,

we can foresee *macroscopic trends*.

We **cannot predict** the future.
But we **can foresee** it.

What do these words mean?

We cannot predict **specific changes**.
However,
we can foresee **macroscopic trends**.

That is what they mean.

That is, we cannot make
quantitative prediction or
concrete prediction.

For example,
within so many years, this will happen.
Its scale will be about this much.

132

However, we can make
directional foresight or
macroscopic foresight.

For example,
the world will move in this direction.
These kinds of trends will appear in society.

That is, we cannot predict ***detailed changes***
that will happen in the future.
But we can foresee ***major trends***
that will occur in the future.

For example, we make a sand pile on the beach,
and pour water on it down from the top.
At that time,
which channels will the water flow down?
No one can predict the channel,
since it depends on chance or fluctuation.
But everyone can foresee one thing clearly.

Water always flows to a lower level.

This is essentially what we call a ***macro view***.

And, by implementing this **macro view**,
we **can foresee** the future.

If so, how can we acquire
this **macro view**?

Rather than learning the *methods* of predicting the future, we should learn the *laws* of world development.

What should we do to acquire
this **macro view**?

It is not enough simply to expand our perspective
or to look into the distant future.

There is one thing that is vital to acquire such a **macro view**.
What is it?

It is *to learn the **laws** of world development*.

By **world** here we mean
all things and beings including
nature, society, human beings.

We should learn the **laws** that explain
how this **world** changes, develops, and evolves.

In other words, it is *the law that states*
all things in the world
will necessarily develop in this direction.

By learning this,
we can foresee the future
through activating this **macro view**.

Up until now, various methods have been proposed
and used to predict the future.
But rather than learning such **methods**
of predicting the future,
something more important and effective exists.

It is *to learn the **laws** about*
how the world changes, develops, and evolves.

If so, how can we learn
these **laws** of world development?

By *studying **philosophy**,*
we can learn them.

Philosophy can discern
the ***basic nature** of the world*.
And it can gain an insight into the *laws*
that lie at the basis of
world change, development, and evolution.

By studying **philosophy**,
we can foresee the future.

If so, what kind of **philosophy** is this?

Ancient philosophy

already

teaches us the *laws* of world development.

It is *dialectic*.

That philosophy teaches us
the **laws** of world change, development,
and evolution.

When hearing the word **dialectic**,
most of people will think of a particular philosopher.

That is the philosopher of German Idealism, **Georg Hegel**.

His philosophy is called *Hegel's Dialectic*.
Among the philosophies created by humanity,
it represents the pinnacle of philosophy
and is the most difficult to understand.
But **dialectic** does not belong only
to Hegel.

In Western philosophy,
its beginning is in
the *Dialogue of Socrates*.

And in modern philosophy,
the German philosopher
Karl Marx's *Dialectical Materialism* and
the French philosopher **Jean-Paul Sartre**'s
Existentialism also includes the philosophy of dialectic.

However, **dialectic** is not just discussed in
Western philosophies.
This **dialectic** is discussed
even in *Eastern philosophies*
having a history of several thousand years.

For example, in the foundations of
Buddhist Thought, there is dialectic philosophy.
The Heart Sutra epitomizes this with the words
"Form itself is emptiness.
Emptiness itself is form."
(Shiki-soku-ze-ku, Ku-soku-ze-shiki).

Taoism, which originated in China,
also discusses dialectic.
It is symbolized by the words
"Yin ultimately is Yang. Yang ultimately is Yin."

Another example is *Zen Buddhism*,
which in Japan
attained the most sophisticated depth.
Actually most of the *koans*, or *Zen riddles*, teach
the ultimate confrontation with contradiction.
Thus we can find many instances of dialectic thinking
in the words of Zen.

The *philosophy of dialectic*

teaches us

the *Five Laws* of the development of the world.

In this way, the **ancient philosophies**
created by humanity
have already taught us the **laws**.

How this world changes, develops, and evolves—
dialectic teaches us these **laws** as
wisdom of humanity from the past.

Now then, what kind of philosophy is **dialectic**?

The purpose of this Part II is to relate this
in a simple style.

At first, I shall introduce the laws of dialectic
as the *Five Laws*.

These laws
are the *laws of world development*
that have been stated in various thoughts
and philosophies
ancient and modern, of the East and the West.

The *Five Laws* of Dialectic

The First Law
The law of development through **spiral process**.

    The world develops as if it were climbing a spiral staircase.

The Second Law
The law of development through **negation of negation**.

    Current **trends** always **reverse** themselves in the future.

The Third Law
The law of development through
transformation from quantity to quality.

    When **quantity** exceeds a specific level,
    the **quality** changes dramatically.

The Fourth Law
The law of development through
interpenetration of opposing objects.

    Things which oppose and compete with each other
    come to resemble each other.

The Fifth Law
The law of development through **sublation of contradiction**.

    Contradiction is the driving force
    for the development of the world.

Now, let us discuss these **Five Laws**.

Chapter One

The World Develops as if It were Climbing a Spiral Staircase.

The First Law

The Law of Development through **Spiral Process**.

The world develops as if
it were climbing
a spiral staircase.

Now then, what is the **first law** of dialectic?

It is
the law of development
through **spiral process**.

This is, in a word, the following law.

The world develops as if
it were climbing a spiral staircase.

That is, the progress and development of
everything in the world
does not proceed ever upward in a straight line.
It all develops in a spiral, in a *circular movement*,
as if climbing a spiral staircase.

That is what this law teaches us.

What then happens in this **spiral development**?

We can understand this if we watch
*people climbing a **spiral staircase**.*

If we look at them from the side,
the people are going up the spiral stairs.
That is, as they proceed to a higher position,
they seem to be ***progressing and developing***.

However, if we look at them from high above,
as the people are climbing up the spiral stairs,
they are going around the stairs once and
returning to their original place.
That is, it looks as if
they seem to be ***reviving and restoring***
to their old position.

But if we look carefully,
they have not simply returned to their original position.
By climbing up the spiral stairs, the people
will certainly *have reached one level higher than before.*

That is the *law of development*
*through **spiral process**.*

Now, if this **spiral development**
is the basic nature and
basic form of all things in the world,
just what will happen as a result?

Progress and development and *revival and restoration* occur simultaneously.

Progress and development *and*
revival and restoration
occur simultaneously.

That is what this law teaches us.

In other words, that means the following.

*The **evolution to the future** and*
regression to the origin *of the world*
occur simultaneously.

Such words as **progress** and **evolution** are
often used in the world.

But when we use these words,
we unconsciously harbor a misunderstanding.

144

Progress and **evolution**
are linear developments towards the future.

Consequently, **progress** and **evolution**
are processes in which old things are discarded.

People always harbor this misunderstanding.

However, neither **progress** nor **evolution**
are simply processes in which new things are born.
Nor are they simply processes that throw out old things.

They are *processes by which old things are
revived with new value added.*

They are also *processes by which old things are
revived with new forms.*

And actually this present age
is replete with examples of this **spiral development**.

This **spiral development**,
if we look at the world around us,
can be seen anywhere we look.

Why is it so?

The Internet revolution

has revived

the *nostalgic business models.*

Because a historical event happened.

It was the *Internet revolution*.

The *Internet revolution* began in the mid-1990s.
It gave birth to many *examples of
this spiral development.*

For example, let us consider
e-commerce which uses the Internet to trade in goods.
Then, what are the advanced business models
that were born from this e-commerce?

The business models are as follows:

The Internet auction.
The reverse auction.

An *auction* refers to a *bidding* method.
It is a method by which,
when selling a product,
the seller gathers many buyers to **bid** on it
and sells to the highest bidder
instead of selling at a fixed price.

A *reverse auction* refers to a *limit price* method.
It is a method by which,
when buying a product,
the buyer indicates the price they are willing to pay
and buys it if a seller appears who accepts that price
instead of buying at a fixed price.

Currently in e-commerce,
there are the great number of people
who use these advanced services
called **auctions** and **reverse auctions**
to buy and sell products.

But if we think about it, we notice something strange.

This is by no means a *new business model*.

Because if we think about it,
these methods of **bidding** and **limit prices**
have been around for a long time.
In the old days,
in the corners of village and town marketplaces,
this trading by **bidding** and **limit prices**
was always going on.

That is, these methods of **auctions** and **reverse auctions**
are by no means **new business models**.

Rather, they are n*ostalgic business models*.

If so, why did these **nostalgic models**
fade from view?

The Internet revolution
has triggered
the *spiral development* of the market.

The reason was *rationalization*.

In other words, it is because,
as capitalism developed,
markets became **rationalized.**

Trading goods by such methods as
bidding and **limit price**—
it was a business custom and was going on daily
in the old days, in village and town marketplaces.

However, as capitalism developed and markets expanded,
markets were no longer just
marketplaces in the corners of towns.
And they became r*egional marketplaces*.
Furthermore, they became *nationwide marketplaces*.
And, along with this development,
bidding and **limit price**
became **inefficient** as well as **non-rational**.

For this reason,
such *inefficient business models disappeared*.

No.
Let us be more precise.

For a time
such **inefficient business models** *disappeared*.

148

But, capitalism developed further,
markets reached a global scale, and
nationwide marketplaces became
worldwide marketplaces.
And as capitalism developed,
the information revolution advanced.
So, ***informatization of the market*** advanced,
and ***rationalization of the market***
developed to its limits.

However, just at that stage,
a revolution occurred that pushed
capitalist development even further.

It was the ***Internet revolution***.

And, through the arrival of this revolution,
oddly enough, the *nostalgic business models* of
bidding and **limit price** were revived in the markets.
In the form of
the **Internet auctions** and **reverse auctions**,
these business models that had once disappeared
came back to life.

Now, what happened?

Spiral development *of the market* happened.

The capitalist market made one turn around
the **spiral staircase**.
For this reason, business models that had once
disappeared were revived.
The nostalgic business models have come back to life.

But here we must realize an important matter.

Spiral development is not simply *revival and restoration.*

Spiral development *is not simply*
revival and **restoration**.

We must realize this.

As stated earlier, **spiral development**
is a development as if climbing a **spiral staircase**.

That is, looking from above,
it seems that we are returning to the same place,
but from the side,
we have actually climbed up one level.
That means *something is definitely*
progressing and developing.

For example, let us consider
the **auctions** and **reverse auctions**
that were revived in e-commerce.
The old methods of **bidding** and **limit price**
have not been **revived** in exactly their original forms.

For sure, they have climbed up one level.
Certainly they have progressed and developed.

That is because
the **bidding** and **limit price** in old markets
could only function at most with
several hundred people.

150

But the **auctions** and **reverse auctions**
that were revived in e-commerce
are markets on the Internet.

For that reason, it is possible to sell and buy goods
targeting ***millions*** and ***billions*** of people on earth.
And as a result of the global distribution revolution,
even people on the other sides of the globe
can trade instantly with
a minimum of time, effort and cost.

This means that
we have climbed up one spiral step.

That is, in this **spiral development**,
we have actually climbed up one level
and something is definitely
progressing and developing.

If we overlook this,
we misunderstand the meaning of **spiral development**.
We would take it as
simple **revival of something old** or
restoration to the past.

We climb up one spiral step.

Actually, this is a *vital perspective*
when foreseeing the future
through the application of
the *law of* **spiral development**.

When there is *revival and restoration,* something necessarily *progresses and develops.*

Let us look at one more example of **spiral development**.

This is the *Net-based group purchase*.

Since the Internet revolution, in e-commerce,
this business model of
the Net-based group purchase has been expanding.
It is the business model by which, when selling goods,
the seller will attract customers by saying that
there would be a 20% discount,
if a hundred people can gather to make the purchase.

Since the Internet revolution, we can see many online shops
that have expanded their sales by using
this system of the **Net-based group purchase**.
However, this is also a *nostalgic business model*.
If we think about it carefully,
this type of *group purchase*
has been around for a long time.

It is the *consumer cooperative* (*or co-op*).

Local people or workers get together to order products
needed for their living.
By doing this, they bring down the product price.
Such a system has existed from long ago.

But, as the distribution revolution has advanced
and price competition has progressed through
volume purchasing by major supermarkets,
such a system of **group purchase** by the **co-op**
has become out of the mainstream in the world.

However, with the emergence of e-commerce,
the *group purchase* system has been revived
as a *Net-based* business model.
That is, it has come back to life.

And, this naturally was not a **simple revival of
something old**.

That is because, in the **Net-based group purchase** system,
which differs from the **co-op** system,
the people participating in group purchases
do not have to belong to special organizations,
or to gather in special localities or workplaces,
and anyone can freely participate by responding to
invitations over the Internet.

In this way,
the emergence of the business model of
the **Net-based group purchase** is also not simply
revival of something old or **restoration to the past**.
Rather,
*it has climbed up one step on the **spiral staircase***.
Something has progressed and developed.

Now then, are these examples of spiral development
occurring only in the *market*?

Not so.

E-learning

has revived

a *nostalgic educational system.*

This **spiral development**
has not only been occurring in the **market**.
It has been occurring in various forms
in the domains of both **society** and **culture**.

If so, in **society**, what kind of
spiral development has been occurring?

For example, in the field of education,
the Internet revolution has spread **e-learning**,
which uses the Internet.
As a result, it has become possible
to receive various kinds of education
at home, at a time of one's choosing.

However, the essence of **e-learning**
is not simply a system of **distance learning**.
If so, what is it?

It is a system of **individualized learning**.

That is, in other words, **e-learning** is
*an educational system where individual learners
can acquire knowledge according to their own
interests and abilities, individually, at their own paces.*

In contrast, in conventional education,
despite learners each having different
interests and abilities,
they were required to follow the same teacher,
the same curriculum, and the same textbook,
and to study at the same pace.

This was a common system called *group education*,
which was conducted
not only in elementary and middle schools
but also in the academies, professional schools
and private seminars.

However, *e-learning*,
having emerged from the Internet revolution,
is a system in which learners can individually and freely
choose fields based on their own interests,
and can learn at their own pace
matching their individual abilities.
That is, learners can search for websites
offering education in subjects of personal interest,
and can select educational services
offering the curricula most suitable for them.
It is an *individualized learning* *system*
where learners are free to choose their learning style
whether to study at a fixed time every day or
to concentrate on their study on a weekend.

And then, if we think about it carefully,
this **individualized learning** system
is a revival of a *nostalgic educational system*.

Why is that?

The regression of an educational system has occurred, from *mass*, *uniform*, and *heteronomous* to *individual*, *free*, and *autonomous*.

That is because
all of the **educational systems** in societies in the past
were **individualized learning** systems.

The **educational systems** in past societies
differed from the present ones.
They were not systems in which
a mass of pupils and students of the same age
gathered, and received education uniformly
following a heteronomous curriculum.

For example, in medieval European society
children of the aristocracy
received education through the *private tutor system*.

This was a system in which
a single teacher was in charge of a single pupil
individually, and offered education freely
following an autonomous curriculum
by taking into account
the interests and abilities of the pupil.

Also, during the feudal age in Japan,
the common people would receive their education
at *temple schools* (*terakoya*).

In this **temple school** system,
people of various ages and social classes
would gather at places such as temples spontaneously,
and study individually and autonomously
based on their interests and abilities.

That is, if we look back at the history of humanity,
the modern educational system by no means has
a long history.

Educational systems that emphasize
the **masses**, **uniformity**, *and* **heteronomy**—
such systems by no means have a long history.

Educational systems that emphasize
the **individual**, **freedom**, *and* **autonomy**—
such systems were, from a historical viewpoint,
the mainstream for a long time.

But, in the transition to modern **industrialized society**,
as the need increased to provide education
efficiently to large numbers of people,
the educational systems that emphasized
the **mass**, **uniform** and **heteronomy**
became the mainstream.

Consequently, the educational systems that emphasized
the **individual**, **freedom** and **autonomy** found in
the **private tutor** and the **temple schools** disappeared.

Old educational systems

have come back

with *new value.*

However,
these old educational systems of the ***private tutors***
and the ***temple schools*** are now coming back
along with the progress and development of society.
They are coming back in the form of ***e-learning***
through the Internet revolution.

That is because, by making use of the Internet,
e-learning realized an educational system in which
everyone can receive ***one-to-one*** *education* at low cost.

Especially, at the beginning,
e-learning was run with e-mail,
but recently, the popularization of broadband
made ***videoconferencing*** possible.
It has enabled us to not only impart ***knowledge***,
but also impart ***tacit knowing*** inexpressible in words.

That is, education through a ***private tuto****r* system,
which could not be offered in the past except to
the aristocracy and wealthy families,
is now *easily obtainable at low cost to everyone*
through e-learning.

158

Also, by utilizing the Internet,
e-learning enables anyone to take advantage of
an educational system where people can learn
at their own pace, in accordance with subjects of
their own interests and abilities.

That is, the education offered in the past through
temple schools and tutors can now be obtained easily
by anyone without having to live in a particular location.

However, this also is a **spiral development**.
It is not just a **revival**.

The e-learning system is not limited
to the knowledge held by a **single private tutor**
or only to the books in a **single temple school**,
but *affords instruction in which people can freely
acquire **knowledge from all over the world**,
and learn from the **best teachers in the world***.

In reality, major universities in the world
such as MIT and Stanford
now provide over the Internet
free movies of their lectures
and anyone can access those lectures.

This is precisely
the *revival of an old educational system
at a sophisticated level.*
It is none other than the ***spiral development** of
the educational system.*

E-mail

has revived

the culture of the *letter*.

Let us take one more example of **spiral development** in society.

It is *e-mail*.

Convenient e-mail is
now used freely by most people in advanced countries.
But if we think about it carefully,
this is a revival of the old *letter*.

In human history in the past,
the **letter** was the major means of communication.
And everyone wrote **letters** to
communicate with people far away.

However, because of the appearance of the *telephone*,
that culture of communication changed.
This is because most people became able to easily use
the **telephone** as a means of communication.

For this reason, the habit of writing **letters**
no longer became mainstream in the world.

Compared to the telephone, the **letter** is a medium
that requires time and effort to write and send.
So this old means of communication came to be
avoided by most people.

But, with the emergence of e-mail,
that *culture of the letter* was revived.

To write messages by *text*
and deliver them to other people—
that *nostalgic culture of communication*
was revived and again became mainstream.

However, this is not a simple **revival**.
This also is a **spiral development**.

That is because
e-mail differs from the **letters** of the past
in some of the following ways:
E-mail can easily be written with
a smartphone or personal computer.
E-mail can reach people anywhere on earth instantly.
E-mail can send the same message to
many people simultaneously.
Furthermore, voice and videos can be sent
by voice mail and video mail.

This is because the culture of the letter has been revived
accompanied by **new values** as mentioned above.

The Internet revolution

has revived

the culture of the *volunteer*.

In this way, what the Internet revolution brought us
was a revival of a **nostalgic thing**
that existed in markets and societies in the past.
It was none other than
a **spiral development** of the world.

And, actually, the Internet itself
came, embracing a *nostalgic culture*.

What is it?

It is the culture of the *volunteer*.

The new medium of the Internet,
from its very beginning,
has embraced the culture of the **volunteer**.
It is a *culture in which*
*people **spontaneously** help and assist each other*
not because of being forced to do so by others
nor being motivated by monetary compensation.

For example, there are the *knowledge communities*
that emerged in great number
owing to the Internet revolution.

These are the **online communities** where
a large number of people
sharing interests in similar topics
gather on the Internet.

In such communities, if someone posts a question,
other participating members in that community
offer various opinions and special knowledge
addressed to that question.
In other words, they offer their valuable *knowledge*.

But, that is not because they have obligation or
responsibility to answer those questions,
nor they expect some kind of monetary compensation for
answering them.
The reason is simply that members feel like assisting
other members who post their questions,
and feel like answering them **spontaneously**.
This is because such a **volunteer** culture,
namely a *mutual assistance culture*,
resides in this community.

However, this **volunteer** culture
residing in the **online community**
is also a **nostalgic culture**.

It is a culture that
always existed in the local communities in the past.
In every area of the world,
there was a *culture in which the people in the region
helped and assisted each other*.
And it was also a *culture of a whole society*.

If so, why did this culture fade from view?

From now on,

a revival of the culture of the *volunteer*

will occur on a worldwide scale.

This is because of the development of capitalism.

The development caused
a massive shift of the working population,
depopulation of rural areas,
and population concentration in large cities.

In the midst of such changes,
the culture of the **volunteer**,
which had its roots deeply in local communities,
was lost.
*The **volunteer** culture, found in all corners of society,
began to disappear.*

However, the Internet revolution
has revived the once-lost **volunteer** culture.
It has revived the culture of the **volunteer** again
all over society through the **online community**.

This is, in a sense,
a ***spiral development** of culture*.

In the past society, the culture of the **volunteer**
spread its roots deeply through the corners of society
along with the activity of
mutual assistance by the people.
However, along with the development of capitalism,
all kinds of services now were becoming ***commodities***.

164

A culture in which all kinds of services were
convertible to *currency* spread widely.
And with this, the **volunteer** culture declined.

But, with the arrival of the Internet revolution,
that **culture** came back to life.
This was precisely
a **spiral development** at the level of **culture**.
The *nostalgic culture* of the past has been revived.

However, again,
this is not a simple **revival** but a **spiral development**.

Because, in this **knowledge community**, people are able to
cooperate with people on the other side of the Earth.
In the old community, mutual assistance was limited to
a few hundred people because of geographical restrictions.
But, in this new community,
millions of people across the globe
can help and assist each other.

The symbolic example of this is the *Linux community*.
It is the knowledge community in which software engineers
around the world gather and continually improve on
the operating system called **Linux**,
which everyone can freely use.
Responding to the invitation of a single engineer,
Linus Torvalds, thousands of engineers are gathering
voluntarily from around the world and
are *offering their knowledge and wisdom*
day and night for no reward.

This is an actual revival of
the **volunteer culture** on a worldwide scale.

Not only *nostalgic things* have been revived, but n*ostalgic things that became convenient* have been revived.

In this way, in markets and in societies,
as well as in the cultural domain,
nostalgic things have been revived.
And a restoration of **nostalgic things** is taking place:

*The business models of the **bidding** and **limit price**.*
*The educational systems of the **private tutor**, and*
*the **temple school**.*
*The cultures of the **letter** and the **volunteer**.*

These are the **nostalgic things** that have been revived.

However, when we look at their **spiral development**,
there is one thing that we must not forget.

The various **nostalgic things**
that are now being **revived**—
they are not merely **nostalgic things**.

They are *nostalgic things that became convenient*.

This must not be forgotten.

Nostalgic things that became convenient—
actually, this viewpoint is extremely important.

That is because, *in markets and societies,*
when **spiral development** *occurs*
and **revival** *of old things happens,*
most of them are revived as
nostalgic things that became convenient.

We should remember again
the law of development through **spiral process**.

In **spiral development,**
we do not merely return to the original point
by going around the spiral staircase.
When we return to the origin,
always we have ascended to a position
one step higher.
Always, something has progressed and developed.

In many cases,
things *have become* **more rational, more efficient**
and **easier to use,** *and have added* **new functions.**
Consequently they **have become more convenient.**

That is, a **nostalgic thing** has returned to **become**
something convenient.

This is what happens in **spiral development**.

Again, this must not be forgotten.

Due to global environmental problems a nostalgic culture of *resource recycling* has been revived.

Now, has such **spiral development**
occurred only in the world of the Internet revolution?

Is it also true that the **spiral development**
has occurred only in such familiar situations as
products and **services** in markets?

Not so.
This **spiral development** has occurred
outside the world of the Internet revolution
in many ways.
This has been occurring on a grand scale
in *social systems*, *political institutions*,
and *economic principles*.

For example, let us take *resource recycling*.

The importance of **resource recycling**
has received strong emphasis,
along with the deepening of
the global warming crisis.
However,
when we look back on history,
this **resource recycling**
also is a revival of an old culture.

In the past,
in ages when economy was relatively undeveloped,
resources were extremely valuable for people.
For that reason, in society
it was a common sense practice to recycle **resources**.
In their daily lives,
people treated resources as precious
and reused them without throwing them away.

But, as economy developed,
and resources became available at low cost,
culture underwent a change.
The so-called
mass-production, mass-consumption culture
became the mainstream.
It was the age of the value system dictating that
mass consumption of resources indicated wealth.

However, the obstacles this kind of society encountered
are *environmental problems* such as global warming.

The consumption of resources on a massive scale
results in the massive discharge of
carbon dioxide into the atmosphere.
As this came to be widely understood,
the *culture of resource recycling* has been revived.

In that sense, this **resource recycling** also
was a regression to the origin of
this old and nostalgic **social system**.

However, after all,
the essence of the regression is **spiral development**,
so, at the same time,
an evolution into the future is also occurring.

Resource recycling at the present time has become a resource recycling that has achieved *spiral development.*

For example, when we look at **resource recycling**
at the individual level,
an evolution into the future is obvious.

In the old days,
if someone recycled needless products and
tried to find people to use them,
finding a person who needed the product
would be very difficult
because it required time, effort and cost to do so.

For that purpose, the only thing that could be done
was to call on one of the few specialists in recycling
or open their own open-air market.
There were no other good methods.

However, at the present time,
in order to carry out such recycling,
an excellent method has emerged.

It is the *flea market.*

By utilizing a flea market service on the Internet,
it is possible to easily discover
someone who needs these items
without spending time, effort, and cost.

Also, inexpensive rapid services have been developed
such as home delivery
for delivering those products to the people who need them.

In this way, in **resource recycling** as well,
regression to the origin *and*
evolution into the future
are taking place simultaneously.
Nostalgic things *are being revived,*
which has become convenient.

This is not only at the individual level.
It can also be seen even in social systems as a whole.

For example, now, in comparison to the past,
there exist high level technologies, systems,
institutions and cultures for resource recycling.

In addition to the **flea market sales system**
mentioned above,
resource recycling has come back with
the following ***new values*** added:

Technology for recycling paper and plastics;
Development of easy-to-recycle eco-materials;
Separate recovery systems for reuse;
Introduction of systems of incentive for reuse;
Heightening of people's awareness of the environment
and the formation of an environmental culture.

In other words, it is a ***revival*** *accompanied by*
new technologies, systems, institutions and cultures.
The old **resource recycling** system has come back
renewed, having achieved spiral development.

Through the Internet revolution
the old and nostalgic *voluntary economy*
has been revived.

Such **spiral development**
has further occurred in **economy** as well.

It is a revival of the ***voluntary economy***.

Now then, what is this **voluntary economy**?

Actually,
it is *the oldest economic principle of humanity*.

In capitalist societies of the present day,
the mainstream is the ***monetary economy***
that is based on **currency**.
For that reason, we unconsciously assume that
the **monetary economy** is the only economic activity.
However, before currency was developed,
humanity was engaged in economic activity.

If so, what kind of economic principles existed
prior to the **monetary economy** based on **currency**?

It was the ***barter economy***
based on the **exchange of goods**.

Now then, what kind of economic principle
existed before this?

It was the **voluntary economy**.

That is the ***gift economy****, in which*
people spontaneously give others items of value
*through **affection** or **goodwill***.
There was an age in which it dominated
human communities and societies.

But, as time passed, the mainstream of economic principles
shifted to the **barter economy**.
And, through the invention of **currency**,
it changed into the **monetary economy**.

However, this does not mean that
the **voluntary economy** disappeared entirely.

*The **voluntary economy** has always played*
a vital role in human history.

For example, activities such as *housework,*
child care, education in the home,
caring for the elderly, community services,
and others were highly important economic activities
although they did not involve an exchange of money.

For example,
society could not function without education in the home,
with only primary and intermediate education.
Without uncompensated care for the elderly
by their family,
public welfare and medical care
would be limited and insufficient.

Two reasons

for the revival of the

voluntary economy.

In this sense, the **voluntary economy**
has been a vital economic principle supporting society,
consistently throughout human history.

But, for two reasons,
this economy has been
in the position of a *shadow economy*.

The first reason is that this economic activity
*was limited strictly to the **narrow domains** of
the family and the locality.*

The second reason is that it actually was **invisible**,
since *it could not be evaluated
by the objective measure of **currency***.

However, this situation changed
when the Internet revolution happened.

*First, in the Internet revolution,
the **voluntary economy** was liberated
from such a **narrow domain**.*

And now, in the domain of the online community,
people can gather from around the world.

And in this community,
people can share their own wisdom
and collaborate with each other.
Furthermore, such activities can influence
the entire world through the Internet.

Secondly, the Internet revolution
*has made **the voluntary economy visible**.*

This cannot be indicated
using the quantitative measure of **currency**,
but it has become visible to many people
by means of the **Internet**.

Now then, what will happen
as a result of this going forward?

*The **voluntary economy***
will expand its influence in a visible form.

In a sense, it is the revival of
the ancient economic principle of community
among humanity.

*The old principle of a **gift economy**,*
as it was called in ancient times,
has been revived through the Internet revolution.
But it has been revived through
a **spiral development carrying new value**.

And this ***voluntary economy*** that has been revived,
in fact, will *evolve into a **new economic principle***
*by merging with the **monetary economy***.

This will be discussed in detail in Chapter Six.

The *spiral development* of things is a subject not only for historians but also for politicians, administrators, and executives.

However, the reader who has read up to this point
most likely harbors one doubt in their mind.

> *Why should we discuss **dialectic** now?*
> *Why should we talk about*
> *the **law of spiral development** now?*
>
> If it is a basic law of development of the world,
> the **spiral development** of things
> would have been occurring since old times.
> The revival of **nostalgic things**
> would have been occurring.
> And many people should have already
> noticed this.
> Nevertheless,
> why should we discuss
> the **law of spiral development** now?

That is exactly correct.
When we look back on world history,
all things have undergone spiral development
from ancient times.

Therefore, outstanding historians,
philosophers and thinkers throughout the world
have had insight into this and spoken about it.

176

However, actually ordinary people
could not see the spiral development.

Because *spiral development up until now*
has occurred on a **historical scale**
over a long period of time.

Consequently, up until now,
this law was an important subject
only for *historians*, *philosophers* and *thinkers*
who observed changes in the world
on a **historical scale**.

For ordinary people
who could observe the world
only at the level of their daily life and work,
it was a law of world development
that they could not notice.

But from this point on, this will change.

It will become an important subject
for *politicians*, *administrators*, and *executives*.

Indeed, it will become an important subject also
for *businesspersons* and *ordinary people*.

Why is this?

Because **symbolic words** are now coming into use.

It has become the age of the *dog year*, and society has begun to run up the spiral staircase.

It is the *dog year*
and the *mouse year*.

That is, changes that used to take 7 years
in the past, now take one year.
Furthermore, changes that used to take 18 years
in the past, now take one year.

As expressed by such words,
the speed of changes in the world
now has accelerated greatly.

As a result, then, what has happened
with these changes?

They have become **visible**.

The spiral developments in the world
have now become visible.

Up until now, spiral developments that occurred
in the world were invisible to most people.

That is because *a **human life** was short*.

For certain, spiral developments have been occurring
since old times.
But these were on the order of several centuries,
taking place very slowly.
So we, as individuals,
could not see these spiral developments.

In other words,
compared to the **lengths of our lives as humans,**
the **speed of spiral developments** *was very slow.*
For this reason, we could not see them.

However, history has now entered
the age of the **dog year**.
And changes in the world
have accelerated considerably.
So, *even in our daily life and work,*
we now can witness **spiral developments** *in the world.*

To use a metaphor,
we are *now* **running up** *the spiral staircase.*

Up until now,
we certainly were climbing up a spiral staircase.
But, since we were climbing up that staircase
much too slowly, over our short lifespan, we were able to
climb up only a few steps of the staircase.
We passed away without even noticing
that it was a spiral staircase.

However, now we are meeting the *age*
in which we **run up** *that spiral staircase.*

For that reason, we can witness various kinds of
spiral developments in our daily life and work.

The age has arrived
when vision, policy, and strategy
immediately become obsolescent.

Therefore, we have met a *new age.*

It is *the age in which we can observe*
*the **spiral development** of the world*
in a single human life.
Moreover, it is *the age in which we witness*
*the **spiral development** of the world*
in our daily lives.

We have met such an age.

However, this fact, on the other hand,
forces politicians, administrators, and executives
to confront a vexing problem.

It is *the problem of*
obsolescence of vision, policy, and strategy.

For example, policies that the government established
by predicting the changes in society and
strategies that companies formulated
by predicting changes in markets
immediately become obsolescent.

They are faced with this problem.

180

The reason for this obviously is the **dog year**.
It is in the fact that the speed of changes
in the world has accelerated.

In the age when changes in the world proceeded slowly,
these changes did not cause great errors,
even if they were considered as **linear changes**.

*On a macro scale, even if it was a **spiral development**,*
on a micro scale,
*it would appear as a **linear development**.*

Because even if we climbed up the spiral staircase,
if we look only at its handrails,
it appears as if the changes were linear.

For this reason,
in government policy and in corporate strategy as well,
we assumed that the tendencies of change
in current society and markets would continue
as before, and even if we assume the current changes
into the future as **linear** extensions, no great errors were
generated from such **predictions**.

However, it is different now,
in the age of the **dog year**.

Compared with the past,
***spiral development** occurs over a short time span,*
*so such **predictions** would not hit their marks.*

According to the spiral staircase metaphor,
we intended to climb to **the east,**
but before we know it
we are climbing to **the west**.

Things that have disappeared have not disappeared because they lost their *reason for existence*.

Consequently, in the age to come where
spiral development will accelerate,
politicians, administrators and executives
formulating their visions, policies and strategies
have to construct their plans by foreseeing
what kind of **spiral development** *will occur*
in society, markets, and the business world,
and *what kind of* **new value** *will be added*,
and *when it will occur*.

If so, how can we foresee such events?

In order to foresee them,
it is necessary to solve *two misunderstandings*
concerning **spiral development**.

Now, what is the first misunderstanding?

Why have the **old things** *disappeared?*

It is a misunderstanding about this question.

Actually, we have a tendency to think
in the following way when something
has disappeared from circulation.

It disappeared
because it lost its **reason for existence**.

However, actually this is not true.
Because, in the midst of changes in an age,
when something disappears from circulation,
the only thing that has disappeared
is its **surface phenomenon**.
It does not at all mean that it has
lost its **reason for existence**.

Hegel instructs us about this with the following words.

Whatever exists, is rational.

What do these words of Hegel tell us?

Whatever actually exists in the world
necessarily has **meaning**.

That is what he tells us.

That is, *out of all the things that existed in this world,*
there is not a single thing
that existed despite having absolutely no **meaning**.
It has merely disappeared from the surface of society,
since the magnitude of its **meaning** has changed
and its relative **importance** has diminished
as time changes and society changes.

It has not disappeared because it lost its **meaning**.
It merely faded away because its
degree of importance *had diminished*.

If so, why has its **degree of importance** declined?

As rationalization and streamlining advance, *older systems* which had once disappeared come back to life.

This is because of *rationalization* and *streamlining*.

When societies, markets and companies,
as well as products and services change in their demand
for **rationalization** and **streamlining**,
among the various **functions** that these have,
functions of high importance are
assigned preference and are strengthened, while
functions of low importance are
abandoned to be realized later, and
occasionally fade from view.

However, as **rationalization** and **streamlining** progress,
functions with a high degree of importance
are fully realized,
therefore the emphasis shifts to **functions**
that had been considered **of**
lower importance up until now.
And a movement arises to bring them into practice.

That is *the reason for their **revival** occurring*.

That is, *when **functions of high importance***
are realized and become widespread,
a chance comes for once disappeared
functions of low importance to be revived.

184

This is the reason why
things that have disappeared come back to life.

The letter and the telephone are examples of this.
The letter has a number of advantages over the telephone.
"We can write while thinking," "we can keep records,"
"we do not interrupt our addressee's time."
These are the advantages it has.
But, it has several disadvantages
compared with the telephone.
"It takes time to write,"
"it takes time to deliver," "a record is left behind."

Consequently,
when we compare these advantages and disadvantages,
in *an age when **promptness** is highly valued*,
the means of communication by letter
lost its major position of importance for a while.
That is why the telephone whose main feature is
promptness came to play a major role.

However, conditions changed with the emergence of *e-mail*.
The *means of communication by letter had
acquired **promptness***, and for this reason,
it was restored to its original major position.

That is, the means of communication by letter
had its own **advantages**, and **reasons for existence**.
But, in the change to a period where
promptness and streamlining are needed,
the **priority order** of its **advantage** declined.
And there was a major shift to the telephone
as a means of communication.

However, with the emergence of e-mail,
featuring promptness and streamlining,
the culture of the **letter** was revived again.

The nationwide uniform distribution revolution

has regressed to

individualism and *regionalism*.

Now let us discuss another case of
the *distribution revolution* in Japan.

This is the *evolution of the convenience store*.

Convenience stores can be found
all over Japan at the present time.
Their history is also a *history of
rationalization and streamlining*.

So, what was the situation
prior to the appearance of the convenience store?

There were many *individual stores* in each region
and a large number of stores existed which
had the *culture of the locality* and
reflected the *personality of the owners*.

However,
under the banner of the distribution revolution,
rationalization and **streamlining**,
the convenience store appeared.
It pursued absolute **rationalization** and **streamlining** of
retail services, through *introducing **information systems***
such as **POS** (point of sale) as well as
the *offering of a nationwide uniform type of service
through the preparation of **operation manuals***.

186

But, in the midst of this distribution revolution,
what disappeared by becoming **hobbled** through this
rationalization and streamlining was
the *individualism* of the small stores, which valued
the individuality of each shop, and the *regionalism*,
in which vendors made their shops reflect local culture.

However, this does not mean at all
that the **reason for existence** for such style
as **individualism** and **regionalism** has been lost.

In order to promote the distribution revolution,
individualism and **regionalism** received a low priority.
And it was demanded as a *top priority* to engage in
rationalization and streamlining and provide
products and services of nationwide uniform quality.

But, as the distribution revolution progressed,
and convenience stores appeared nationwide,
now that **rationalization** and **streamlining** have
adequately progressed in these shops, there has been
a revival of the **individualism** and **regionalism**.

Because the most advanced convenience stores in Japan
have now begun to engage in creating shops that reflect
the environment of the towns and incorporating
the owners' ideas to add character to the shops.

But the revival of **individualism** and **regionalism**
does not mean simply that
the traditional local shops have been revived.
After all, what has been revived is a *new kind of
individualism and regionalism*, which has achieved
spiral development through implementing
leading edge information systems and operating manuals.

Functions which had once disappeared due to *rationalization* and *streamlining* will be necessarily revived.

So what happened?

Here also, functions that had once disappeared
due to **rationalization** and **streamlining**
came back to life,
since **rationalization** and **streamlining**
had reached a certain stage.

Now, what happened
from the *viewpoint of dialectic*?

It was *the **spiral development** of
homogenization and **individualization**.*

That is what has happened.

In the beginning, the stores, which once had an
individual character in each region and shop,
*aimed at nationwide **homogenization***
in the midst of the rationalization and streamlining
stemming from the distribution revolution.

However, since this **homogenization**
progressed to a certain stage,
it went around the spiral staircase and
*headed again in the direction of **individualization**.*

188

That is, it went through the following
spiral development process:
*Homogenization in order to achieve **rationalization**.*
*Reversal at the end point of **rationalization**.*
*Regression from **homogenization** to **individualization**.*

And this kind of phenomenon of **spiral development** of
homogenization and **individualization**
could be seen not only in the convenience store
but also everywhere in society and markets.

In general, when seeing society and markets
from a macro view, it often happens that *things which*
*once disappeared in the need for **rationalization**,*
move again in the direction of revival
*when **rationalization** reaches its end point.*

If so, when something disappears
through a widespread change,
we should not conclude that
it disappeared because it lost its reason for existence.

Rather, we should deeply consider
the **meaning** and **reason for existence** of
what has disappeared.

Because, by doing this, we will be able to see.

*What will be **revived** going forward?*

The **future** will become visible to us.

In *evolution,*

old things do not disappear.

They coexist and live with *new things.*

Now, what is the second misunderstanding
with regard to **spiral development**?

*What is **evolution**?*

It is a misunderstanding about this question.

The word **evolution** originally is a *term from biology.*
And, it does not mean merely **continuous changes**,
but *discontinuous jumps*.

Recently, also regarding societies, markets and companies,
due to the fact that they have achieved dramatic changes,
it is common to use this word for such things as
evolution into a knowledge society,
evolution into a customer-centric market and
evolution into a social contribution company.

However, the use of the word **evolution** here in this way,
when referring to
societies, markets and companies,
and even to products and services,
regrettably is accompanied by
one misunderstanding.

In **evolution**,
old things disappear.
And **new things** replace them.

That is the *misunderstanding*.

However,
in considering the meaning of the word **evolution**,
we must also understand one more important matter.

That is because, in the process of **evolution**,
actually, one more major thing occurs,
not from the perspective of
the *evolution of individual biological species*,
but from the perspective of
the *evolution of ecosystems as a whole*.

*In **evolution**,
old things do not disappear.
They coexist and live with **new things**.*

We must not forget this.

The process of **evolution** is the same,
not from the perspective of
the **evolution of individual technologies and products**,
but from the perspective of
the **evolution of markets and societies as a whole**.

If so, what does this mean?

In the *evolution of the book,*

it is not the case that all *paper books* disappear

and are replaced by *electronic books.*

To explain the meaning of this expression,
let us look at one easy-to-understand case.

It is the ***evolution of the book.***

In the course of the information revolution,
a revolution is progressing even in the world of
book publishing.
In particular, digitization of the book is advancing
and the technology of the ***electronic book*** is
spreading rapidly.

The **electronic book** is a book
that can be downloaded over the Internet
and read on an easily viewable liquid crystal display.

This is attracting much attention as
the ***future evolution*** of the book.

Old ***print media,***
such as books, magazines and newspapers,
are now moving towards
new ***electronic media***, which are digitized and
sold on the Internet.
This is a very rational direction to follow,
as well as an inevitable one.

This is because **electronic media**
have the following merits:

No cost for production and storage.
No need of effort and time for sale and purchase.
Easy to search and select what one wants.

For these reasons, the **electronic book**
will certainly become popular.
But at the same time,
one important misunderstanding frequently occurs.

In the future, all paper books will become
electronic books,
and all printed media will become
electronic media.

That is the *misunderstanding*.

However, this never will happen.

Actually, even 100 years going forward,
paper books and publications will remain.

That is because paper books and publications
have their own **rationality**
for their existence.

In the evolution of living things,
both *old species* and *new species*
coexist together on earth.

For example,
its rationality is in the **pleasure** of reading a book.

If we avail ourselves of a book that has classical value,
as we read through it,
enjoying the touch of the paper,
the turning of each page,
we bend our ear deeply to the voice of the author,
converse with one who is so far away,
and engage in a dialogue with our inner self.
Sometimes we are inspired to underline the text
when it strikes us, to make notes in the margins,
and after we finish reading a book,
we close the cover and
are overcome with deep emotion for a while.

This *pleasure of reading a book*
is part of the wonders of a *paper book*,
and we cannot replace it with anything else.

Of course, even in *electronic books*,
a function for turning pages is included.
Also, there are functions for marking and writing notes.
But, after all,
it is close but not the same as a **paper book**.

194

Consequently, no matter how widely popular
electronic books may become,
the **paper book** will never disappear.

Both of them necessarily will
differentiate from each other and coexist side-by-side.

This actually is clear when we observe
the shape of ***evolution*** *in the world of nature.*

In Darwin's theory of evolution,
fishes became amphibia,
which in turn evolved into reptiles,
and reptiles into mammals,
and the primates developed from mammals.

And among these primates, apes evolved from monkeys,
and Homo sapiens developed from apes.

However, if we look back on
this grand process of evolution,
even now on the Earth,
fishes, amphibia, reptiles, mammals, monkeys and
human beings all exist.

And all these *various forms of life*
differentiate from each other and coexist side-by-side
on the Earth.

Of course, sometimes some species may
be naturally selected and disappear.
However, the shape of **evolution** in the world of nature
is moving in such a direction that *species increasingly*
undergo ***diversification****.*

The essence of *evolution* is *diversification.* The world increases in *diversity.*

This is the essence of **evolution**.

That is, the *essence of **evolution** is **diversification**.*

In **evolution**,
it is not true that **old things** simply disappear
and **new things** replace them.

*It is a process by which **old things** from the past and*
***new things** that have just come to life,*
by differentiating from each other and
coexisting side-by-side,
*have heightened the **diversity of the world**.*

Even if several **older forms** become
extinct through selection at times,
from a macro view, the world moves towards
diversification based on coexistence.
And as a result, *the world becomes*
*increasingly **rich in life**.*

If so, what happens if we apply this concept to
evolution of products in markets?

The **evolution of products** in markets
does not simply mean that an **old product** disappears
and a **new product** takes the majority of market share.
These differentiate from each other and
coexist side-by-side in the same way as living species.
Therefore, both the **paper book** and the **electronic book**
will differentiate and coexist.

The *paper book* will most likely live on
as a medium suitable for
perusing long-favorite classics,
reading favorite poems savoring their word,
and keeping them close at hand.

The *electronic book* will most likely gain
in popularity as a medium suitable for
the information in dictionaries and encyclopedias
that require search functions,
the recent information that is required
through constant updates,
and the practical data that we need not keep.

In this way, the *evolution of products* in markets,
seen in a broader perspective, is none other than
diversification of the product ecosystem.

Both **new** and **old products**
differentiate from each other and coexist side-by-side.

In other words,
it means that
the market and society increase in diversity
and become a *rich market* and a *rich society*.

In observing society,

we should consider what is *nostalgic*

and what *became convenient*.

Now, as we have discussed up to now,
in order to foresee the future
by applying the law of **spiral development**,
there are two things we must
understand correctly.

*Why do **old things** fade from view?*

*What is **evolution**?*

When we have understood these two correctly,
we can confront the following two questions.

How can we witness **spiral development** in the world?
How can we make use of this **law of spiral development**?

Now then, first of all,
*how can we witness **spiral development** in the world?*

To begin, we must ***observe society***.

For example,
we must see *the most recent trends* and *hit products*.
We must see *new social systems* and *new institutions*.

In doing so, we will likely discover
nostalgic things that became convenient
among the various things we see.

At such a time, we should think deeply about them.

*What is **nostalgic**?*
*What has **become convenient**?*

When thinking about this,
the **essence** of changes in the world will appear.
The **future** of changes in the world will appear.

Secondly,
how can we make use of
*this **law of spiral development**?*

Now, in all corners of society or markets,
the **spiral development** of dialectic is occurring.
If this is so,
how can we utilize this **law of spiral development**?
How can we utilize this **law**
to foresee and create the future?

For this purpose,
when scrutinizing the world around us
and things around us,
we should try thinking based on the *four steps*.

We can foresee

the *nostalgic things* that will be revived in the world

by the *law of spiral development*.

Now, what are the **four steps**?

First, *we should foresee **what will be revived***.

This is step one.
As mentioned often up to now,
the **law of spiral development**
states that **evolution into the future** and
regression to the origin occur simultaneously
in the processes of change, development and evolution of
society and markets.
So, when we scrutinize these processes,
we can see a **revival** of **nostalgic things**.
Consequently, we should first foresee
what will be revived.

And what should we do for this?

*We should see **what has disappeared***.

That is step two.
The fundamental direction of events occurring
in the progress and development of society and markets
is **rationalization** and **streamlining**.

Consequently, we should consider **what has disappeared**
in the flow of this **rationalization** and **streamlining**.
We should consider what has disappeared
for not being **rational** or **efficient**.

Having considered **what has disappeared**,
what should we do next?

*We should consider **why it has disappeared**.*

This is step three.
We should consider, at **this stage** of the progress and
development of society and markets,
why it has disappeared.
Also we should consider,
at **that stage,** why it was not **rational**,
and why it was not **efficient**.

If we understand **what has disappeared** and
why it has disappeared
in the flow of **rationalization** and **streamlining**
in society and markets,
and understand **what will be revived**,
then, finally, what should we consider?

*We should consider **how we can revive them**.*

This is step four.
We consider how we can **revive**
what disappeared in the flow of
rationalization and **streamlining**
by using recently developed technologies,
systems and institutions.

This is how to apply the **law of spiral development**.

A new medium
will emerge by merging
the functions of *telephone* and *e-mail*.

Concretely, what should we do?
Let us consider a practical *exercise to apply* the law.

For example, let us take *e-mail*.

There is no need to say this again, but
what has emerged in the flow of the **rationalization** and
streamlining of communication in society, is **e-mail**.

Certainly, through the popularization of **e-mail**,
our communication has become extremely convenient.
This is because the **telephone**, which had been
our main means of communication up until now,
had several disadvantages:

"We cut into the time of the addressee."
"We have to take notes with one hand."
"It is difficult to share information with a third party,
since the information disappears on the spot."

These are the disadvantages.

In contrast,
e-mail has the following advantages:

"We can read it when we want to,
so we do not need to cut into the time of the addressee."
"We communicate by text,
so we do not need to take notes."
"It is easy to share information with a third party
by forwarding the mail."

Above all else,
it has the advantage of **low-cost**,
and thus it was rapidly popularized
in place of the **telephone**.

In this way, **e-mail**, which has now become the mainstream,
is certainly a more **rational** and **efficient** means
in comparison with the **telephone**.
But if we look closely at changes in
our communication patterns by the emergence of **e-mail**,
we notice that
the advantages the **telephone** had **are disappearing**
because of the popularization of e-mail.

If so, what **has disappeared**?

It was the ***nuances of messages***.

By replacement of the **telephone** with **e-mail**,
it has become difficult to convey
the nuances of messages.

Further *spiral development* will occur with the *telephone* as a means of communication.

That is, since the **telephone** is a means of communication
by **voice**, it can convey the **emotion of the voice**,
and so it could communicate **delicate nuances**.

Meanwhile, since **e-mail** is communication by **text**,
it cannot convey the **emotion of the voice**,
and therefore,
it has the disadvantage of being difficult to convey
such **delicate nuances**.

Certainly through the spread of **e-mail**,
communication has become convenient,
but the advantage of the **telephone** by which
we can convey the **emotion of the voice** has disappeared.

So what we should now consider is *how we can **revive**
these **disappeared advantages**
through new technologies and methods.*

For example, then, another technology of communication
that integrates the advantages of
both the **telephone** and **e-mail**
may be revived, along with further evolution.

For example, it is
video mail with text conversion function.

The elemental technology
to realize this communication method already exists.
It is such a following communication method that,
when you speak a message at a camera on your smartphone
and ask the AI on the smartphone
to send the message to a certain friend,
the AI sends an e-mail with your video message to them.

Then, the receiver of the e-mail can, on their smartphone,
not only see your message as a video message
but also hear it as a voice message.
Furthermore, thanks to AI's text conversion function,
the receiver can also read your message as a text message.

This is
not only the merging of traditional **telephone** and **e-mail**,
but also additional integration of **videophone**,
which is none other than a further *spiral development* of
our means of communication.

Of course, this **video mail with text conversion function**
has an advantage:
"We do not need to cut into the time of the addressee."
In contrast, however, it cannot provide **real-time dialogue**.
In addition, it also has advantages:
"We do not need to take notes."
"It is easy to share information."
In contrast, however, there is
the *issue of psychological resistance*:
"The message will remain as voice or video data."

However, I would like you to remember.
Evolution means diversification.
We will wisely select the proper option
out of various means of communication,
which have evolved and diversified,
to use depending on our needs at different times.

Chapter Two

Current *Trends*
Always *Reverse* Themselves in the Future.

The Second Law

The Law of Development through
Negation of Negation.

Current *trends*
always *reverse* themselves
in the future.

As we discussed in the previous chapter,
the things around us go on to achieve **spiral development**.
Let us look at the appearance of this development
from a slightly different viewpoint.

We should look at it
not from **the viewpoint of** *function*
but from **the viewpoint of** *trend*.

First, when we look at this spiral development
from the viewpoint of **function**,
it looks as if a function that had disappeared
has been **revived**.
Then, if we view it from the viewpoint of **trend**,
what do we see?

We see a *reversal*.

It looks
as if a **reversal** has happened to the previous **trend**.
That is, *the trend of changes up to this point*
now goes in an opposite direction.

In other words, this is *a **rebound** of a **trend***.

If we consider **trends** in changes in the world,
they necessarily cause **rebounds**
in the opposite direction.

Just like a ball thrown against a wall
is jumping back after hitting the wall,
a **rebound** takes place.

Actually, there is another **law** in dialectic
that teaches us this.

It is
the law of development through
negation of negation.

That is,

*Current **trends***
*always **reverse** themselves in the future.*

That is the law.
To state this more simply,
things develop by *two occurrences of **negation***.

That is, at first, some things begin to change
by being **negated**,
and at their end point,
that **negation** is **negated** once more,
and a new development arises.

However, the **negation** we are talking about here
is *not a **mechanical negation***
*but a **dialectical negation**.*
It never has the sense of **erasing** or **destroying**,
rather it *exceeds*, or *transcends* that stage.

Competition in *low-cost services* always rebounds in the direction of competition in *knowledge services*.

Now, let us examine one example of this.

It is ***online trading***.

This is a service which makes it possible to trade in stocks using the Internet, and it is clear why this business model emerged and expanded so dynamically.

This is because the trading fees in the business model of conventional stockbrokerage firms were too expensive.

If so, why were these fees expensive?

Because in conventional stockbrokerage firms, the focus of service was **face-to-face** meeting by contact persons or salespersons.

That is, the business model of **face-to-face** meetings that not only offered ***transaction services*** for stock trading but also offered ***information services*** such as the latest trends in the market and advice on stock trading. For this reason, operating costs were high, as were trading fees.

In contrast to this, the online stockbrokerage firms,
which offered **online trading** services,
had *abandoned* the conventional brokerage practice of
face-to-face information services.
And because they *restricted* it to
transaction services of stock trading over the Internet,
the operating costs were very low, and they could also
sharply reduce the trading fees.

This is the main reason why
the online brokerages expanded so rapidly.

In a sense, this means that
the online brokerages grew rapidly
because they *negated the competition for*
the conventional ***face-to-face information services***
and engaged strictly in competition
for ***low-cost trading services***.

This is the *first* **negation**.

However, in this field of **online trading**,
numerous companies began to participate
in a very short period of time,
a large number of the online brokerages appeared,
and **price wars** intensified.
For this reason, *trading fees*
had reached their lowest point.

It was a condition of so-called ***price collapse***.

And, what happened in this condition was
precisely the **rebound**.

At some stage,

price competition **always reverses to**

value-added competition.

This is because in the midst of this price competition
surging to its limit,
many online brokerages began *shifting their strategies.*

They began to move their main battlefield
from *price competition* involving competing for
low-cost trading services
to *value-added competition* involving competing for
advanced information and knowledge services.

That is,
the **rationalization** and **streamlining** of online trading
advanced to their limits,
and at the stage where **price competition**
based on cost reduction reached its limit,
a **reversal** occurred.
That is, a **rebound** occurred.

This is the *second **negation**.*

*The **price competition***
that began earlier in the form of
*negating **information service competition***
*underwent a **reversal** in the direction towards*
information service competition
*now in the form of negating **price competition**.*

This is an example of the law of
development through **negation of negation**.

Of course, this newly emerging **information service**
resulting from **negation of negation** was not
a revival of an earlier **face-to-face information service**.
It had evolved by **ascending one more step
on the spiral staircase**.

By utilizing the Internet or information technology,
the **information and knowledge services** at this new stage
have become much more **convenient** for the customer
in the sense of *rapidity, accuracy, comprehensiveness,
searchability, and bidirectionality.*

And this **development through negation of negation**
is not occurring only in the field of **online trading**.
In the coming age, it will occur in other domains as well.

First, *in some domains, new entry companies will emerge
and thus an all-out **price competition** will begin*
by negating the ways of the existing
inefficient, highly priced services.
*But when the **price competition** reaches its limit,
it will shift to **value-added competition** of services
by negating the **price competition**.*

For example, for the customer, this will involve
knowledge services *offering rich knowledge and wisdom,*
mind services *offering warmth and consideration and*
one-to-one services *with full consideration of the customer.*

Value-added competition based on
offering such services will begin.
And such a **reversal** through **negation of negation**
will become a phenomenon to be always witnessed in
many domains of business
where rationalization is progressing.

In the *knowledge society*,

knowledge expressible in words will lose its value and *wisdom* inexpressible in words will acquire value.

Now, let us look at one more example of
the **reversal** and **rebound**.

It is the *paradox of the knowledge society*.

If we ask, **"what kind of society
will we have in the future?"**
many people will answer,
a knowledge society.

If so, what kind of society will this be?
In answer to this question, surely many people
will reply, **a society in which knowledge has value**.

But in reality, *a knowledge society
is a society in which knowledge loses its value*.

Because this **knowledge society**,
if we look at it in greater depth,
will appear to develop spirally.

First, in society prior to the knowledge society,
the media had not developed much,
so ordinary people could not easily acquire
specialist knowledge or recent knowledge.
Therefore, these types of knowledge carried a *high value*.

However, with the advent of the Internet revolution,
many people acquired terminals such as
smartphones and personal computers,
and communication costs dropped dramatically.
Moreover, every day, enormous amounts of information
were made public on websites,
and countless knowledge communities
were born on the Internet.

For that reason, in the new coming age,
knowledge expressible in words _itself will be_
available to everyone without effort, time and cost.
So _the **knowledge expressible in words**_
representing specialist knowledge or recent knowledge
ends up losing its relative value.

This means that we will have
a society in which knowledge has lost its value.

Now then, if **knowledge expressible in words**
is losing its value, what is coming to have value?

It is **_wisdom inexpressible in words_**.

For example, **wisdom inexpressible in words**
such as _skills, senses, techniques_ and _know-how_,
will come to have great value
in the knowledge society that is emerging.

This precisely
is spiral development of the knowledge society.

The *age of knowledge*
is ending
and the *age of wisdom* is beginning.

This is because *in earlier societies,*
wisdom inexpressible in words *had great value.*

For example, in the workplace for apprentices,
as expressed by the words "learn with your body" and
"grasp it with your breath,"
the **wisdom** of skills, senses, techniques and know-how
had great value.
Such **wisdom** could not be expressed by words,
and they were things that were impossible
to communicate or acquire easily.

However, through the *invention of printing technology*,
mass media was born.
This mass media, which made it possible to
communicate **knowledge expressible in words**
to many people, enabled them to share and utilize
specialist knowledge and recent knowledge.
And in this way, mass media improved
the productivity of society as a whole,
created a rich culture
and promoted the development of society.

However, even at this stage,
in order to learn **knowledge**, people needed
schools, *which restricted them in place and time,*
or ***books***, *which needed cost and time for distribution.*

For this reason, **knowledge expressible in words**
had a high value in society at that stage.

But then, the Internet revolution occurred.

This revolution realized a *personal media*
that surpasses mass media, and anyone,
as long as they had a terminal
such as a smartphone or personal computer,
could easily acquire
specialist knowledge and recent knowledge.

As a result, **knowledge expressible in words** lost
its relative value, and *in a new dimension,*
wisdom inexpressible in words
again acquired great value.

In this way, if we look back on history up to the time of
the **knowledge society**, *the earlier **age of wisdom***
*developed into the **age of knowledge**.*
But, since sharing of knowledge became easier
through the Internet revolution,
a **reversal** and **rebound** occurred,
and now the age of knowledge is moving in the direction of
*an **age of wisdom** in a new dimension.*

This is also an example of
development through negation of negation.

The trend towards *high-tech* necessarily rebounds towards *high-touch*.

In this way, when we look at the world,
we notice that this law of
development through negation of negation
is happening universally.

This trend very much resembles
the movement of a **pendulum**.

The world seems to change
*in the same way as a **pendulum**.*

That is, when the world changes in a certain direction,
when it reaches its end point,
it begins to move in the opposite direction.
And if we understand this,
we can acquire a ***macro view***.

For example, in which direction is
high-tech society moving?

It is clear, if we consider this **pendulum**.

*The trend towards **high-tech**, at its end point,*
*will necessarily move in the direction of **high-touch**.*

This is what we will notice.

Societies that are pursuing **high-tech** by
making use of leading edge science and technology,
at its end point, will necessarily move
in the direction of a society which highly values
high-touch, that is, care and concern for people.

For example, this is quite clear if we examine
the successful cases of the *online shops*
at the initial stage in Japan.

In the beginning,
in order to make the **online shops** successful,
high-tech was considered to play a key role, such as
the introduction of electronic transaction systems,
clear displays of product images, and
development of product databases.
However, when we view the development of
the online shops that followed this,
most of the successful shops
had not only introduced **high-tech**, but, in fact,
they made use of e-mail, and customer communities,
creating establishments that greatly valued
high-touch with their customers.

In this way, by pursuing **high-tech**, at its end point,
the pendulum necessarily begins to move
in the direction of **high-touch**.

And, behind this trend
there are two laws of dialectic:
the law of development through **spiral process** and
the law of development through **negation of negation**.

We should understand this.

The *dialectic worldview*
existed
also in ancient Eastern philosophy.

However, as I mentioned in Foreword,
this **dialectic** was by no means
an **original idea** of Hegel's philosophy or of
Western philosophy.

Actually, this **dialectic worldview** existed
also in *Eastern philosophy* since long ago.

For example, the following words in ***Taoism***
teach us that.

"Yang ultimately is Yin."
"Yin ultimately is Yang."

These words in Taoism mean that
changes in things, at their end point,
undergo reversal.
And Eastern philosophy had discerned
this fact since long ago.

Also, this law of dialectic
is related in various words
in Eastern philosophy.

For example, let us consider these words:

**"The Great Self (*Taiga*) resembles
the Non Self (*Muga*)."**

When the hearts of humans
move in the direction of realizing
the great ideal called *Taiga* (the Great Self), strangely,
they approach the boundaries of *Muga* (the Non Self).
That is what these words teach us.

Also, *when humans age,
becoming **elderly** at a mature state of being,
for some reason, they return to the world of innocence
and ingenuousness, like an **infant***.
The famous Japanese Zen master **Ryokan**
undertook severe disciplinary training from a young age,
and reached a deep state of being.
In his old age, as legends have it,
he was moving in the direction of playing innocently
with little children, and having a good time.

Also, in Japan where everything is considered as
a ***path*** to the *world of the spirit of Zen*,
even in the world of fishing,
we can speak deeply of the ***Tao of fishing***.
And in this world there is the saying:

"Fishing begins with carp, and fishing ends with carp."

This is also none other than the words suggesting
development through spiral process.

If we look around carefully, we can see that the world of
Eastern philosophy abounds in the laws of dialectic.

When we apply dialectic thinking, we can foresee the next *main battlefield* and it serves us in *strategic thinking*.

Up to this point we have been discussing
two laws of dialectic:
the law of development through **spiral process** and
the law of development through **negation of negation**.

When understanding this, the readers
naturally harbor one new question in their mind.

> *If so, how can we take advantage of these laws*
> *in implementing actual change?*

That is the question.

At this point, let us discuss just *how we can*
*implement these laws in **strategic thinking**.*

Up until now, we have discussed how important it is
to foresee the **revival** of functions which had disappeared
as well as the **reversal** in current trends, by applying
the law of development through **spiral process** and
the law of development through **negation of negation**.

What does it mean, from the viewpoint of
strategic thinking, to foresee these
revivals and **reversals**?

It means that *foreseeing the next **main battlefield***.

For example, by discerning
the **spiral development** in society and markets,
foreseeing what will be **revived**
and what direction will they **reverse** to going forward
is to discern the next direction of competition
between states and between companies.
It is also to discern where
the current **main battlefield** will shift to next.

As mentioned earlier, in the ages before the **dog year**,
changes in the world were unhurried,
as was the shift to a new main battlefield.
Consequently, in **strategic thinking** for states
and companies, there was no need to be concerned
about **where the next main battlefield would be**.
It was sufficient to consider only the strategies
for the **current main battlefield**.

However, in the age of the **dog year** going forward,
changes in the world are stormy,
and shifts in the main battlefields are very rapid,
so in strategic thinking, we must constantly be concerned
about where the **next main battlefield** will be.
Without considering
*what will be the **next main battlefield**,*
we cannot formulate a strategy.

In order to consider this,
let us discuss an important example.

It is an insight into the direction which
the **main battlefield** of market competition
will move into because of the Internet revolution.

The Internet revolution has triggered not only a simple *rationalization of the market* but also the *evolution of the market.*

When asked
"what will happen because of the Internet revolution?"
executives will unanimously reply
with the words:

Rationalization, streamlining and **cost reduction.**

That is, many executives today believe that
the essence of the Internet revolution is **rationalization**
and **streamlining** of company, markets and society,
and **cost reductions** through them.

However, this belief is unfortunately in error.
The *essence of the Internet revolution*
is not such a **rationalization.**

If so, what is it?

*It is **evolution**.*

For example,
what happens through the Internet revolution is
not just the **rationalization of the market**
in the sense that market transactions become rapid
and accurate at low cost.

What happens through the Internet revolution is
that *the nature of the market itself undergoes
a fundamental change*; one that should be called
evolution of the market.

Now then, what is this **evolution of the market**?

It is *an evolution from the **company-centric market**
to the **customer-centric market**.*

That is,
most of the business models in markets up until now
were constructed as ***company-centric***.
But as a result of the Internet revolution,
all of the business models going forward
will be transformed into ***customer-centric*** ones.

For example, let us take the ***auction*** or ***reverse auction***
that we have described earlier.

This is a business model in which *the prices of products,
which have been determined on the **company side** up until now,
are determined on the **customer side**.*

Also let us consider the ***Net-based group purchase*** model.
From the viewpoint of the **customer**,
this is a business model in which
*the **customers** gather, raise their voices
and demand discounts from the **company***.

And the essence of the Internet revolution is
the evolution of the market as a whole
from **company-centric** to **customer-centric**
through recombination of such business models.

In the *customer-centric market* an evolution of the *middleman* will occur through spiral development.

Now, what will happen in this evolved
customer-centric market?

A dialectic **development through spiral process** will occur.
An **evolution through negation of negation** will occur.

To state it concretely, what will the evolution be?

It is the *evolution of the middleman*.

In markets, the **middleman**,
through a dialectic process,
will evolve from an **old middleman** to a **new middleman**.

What kind of process is this?

Just about when the Internet revolution began in the US,
many people replied as follows to the question
"what will now happen to markets?"

"The middleman will die."

Actually because of the Internet revolution,
disintermediation occurred, in which
those **middlemen** were bypassed, who conventionally
did retailing and wholesaling, because it became easy
for producers to sell directly to consumers.
And many middlemen were selected out.

However, in this **customer-centric market**,
within a few years,
something happened that most people had not anticipated.
Several years after the Internet revolution occurred,
people began saying:

"The middleman never dies."

That is because the **middleman** is revived in markets.
However, this was not the old-fashioned type of middleman.
Rather, an entirely new type of middleman appeared,
called *the new middleman*.

If so, what is the difference between
the **old middleman** and the **new middleman**?

The direction that they face is different.
The **traditional middlemen**,
such as retailers and wholesalers,
faced towards the company and
engaged in a business model *based on sales agency*,
while the **new middleman** *faces towards the customer*
and engages in a business model *based on*
purchasing agency.

Now most of the companies called
online businesses actually follow
the business model of the **new middleman**.

The *middleman* who once was negated will come back in the form of the *new middleman*.

For example, **amazon.com**, which grew rapidly
in the world of the online business,
is not only a company functioning
as a **sales agency** for books over the Internet.
Actually this company *serves* to offer
purchasing agency to the reader.

This is because the amazon sites,
responding to the needs of the readers,
offer many services such as the following:

Confirming availability and time of delivery.
Searching for used books.
Auctioning unneeded items.
Introducing related books.
Providing reviews of books.

And this is the **new middleman**,
who offers comprehensive services of
both the **purchasing agency** and **purchasing support**
in order to make available to the readers
what they are seeking.

And if we examine
the essence of this company,
we see that not only amazon
but most online businesses actually follow this
new middleman business model.

And the Internet revolution thus *has brought about*
*the evolution from the **old middleman***
*to the **new middleman*** in markets.
This process of the evolution of the middleman
is also the dialectic process of
development through negation of negation.

That is, in the very beginning, in the flow of
rationalization through the Internet revolution
the **disintermediation** occurred.
As the words "the middleman will die" suggest,
the old middleman was selected out
and was **negated**.

However, soon in markets,
along with the words "the middleman never dies,"
the middleman, who was **negated**,
has been **revived**.

The middleman has been **revived**
as a new occupation called the **new middleman**.

Certainly, this is the process of
development through negation of negation.

*The once **negated** middleman*
has been revived as the new middleman
*through **negation of negation**.*

By using dialectic thinking,

we can adopt the *strategy of preemption*

by foreseeing the *revival* and *reversal*.

This is the **evolution of the middleman**
in the customer-centric market.

And if we gain an insight into
the **next evolution** of this middleman,
we can see the ***next main battlefield*** clearly.

It is *the battlefield that involves*
the position of the **new middleman**.

That is, in the **customer-centric market**,
the **new middleman**, who is offering such services as
purchasing agency and **purchasing support**
from the standpoint of the customer,
will quite naturally gather strong empathy
from the customer and seize leadership in the market.

Consequently, in each market,
competition will begin centered on
the position of the **new middleman**
having the most trust from the customers.

Who will become
the first new middleman in that market?
Who will become
the strongest new middleman in that market?
Which new middleman should we tie up with?

Competition will start from
the consideration of these issues.

So if we understand deeply
the law of **spiral development** and
the law of **negation of negation**,
and if we gain an insight into
the answers to the following questions:
    In the markets going forward,
    what will be **revived**?
    In which direction will **reversals** occur?
    Where will the **main battlefield** move towards next?
then, we can naturally decide the strategy to take.

Now, at such a time, what kind of strategy do we need?

It is ***the strategy of preemption***.

What should we do if we figure out
where the **main battlefield** will move towards next?

We should *preempt to that next main battlefield*
and *establish a strategic **foothold** earlier than others*.

For example, if we gain an insight into
the **evolution of the middleman**,
we should begin the business model of the **new middleman**
ahead of others in that market.
We should emerge as
the first **new middleman** in that market.

This is the strategy of **preemption**.

In the age of the dog year
strategic thinking evolves
because *strategic wait time* is reduced.

And in this age of the **dog year**,
this strategy of **preemption** will become
extremely effective.

Why is this?

Because *the **wait time** is short*.

In the age of the **dog year**,
the **wait time** to move into
the **next main battlefield** is short.

Conversely, in ages prior to the **dog year**,
even if we adopted a strategy of **preemption**,
market changes were slow-paced,
so the *strategic wait time* became too long.
For this reason, it exceeded the *strategic endurance time*
determined by the relationship of
the financial and organizational ability of the company,
in many cases,
resulting in their *inability to wait any longer*.

But in the future we will enter the age of the **mouse year**,
which surpasses the **dog year**.
And the **main battlefield** in the market
will shift very rapidly.

Therefore, even if we foresee
the **next main battlefield**, it is too late.
Sometimes we must even foresee
the **one after the next main battlefield**.

So, let us consider the shift of the **main battlefield**
from the **old middleman** to the **new middleman**.
Where will the next **main battlefield** be after that?

We shall discuss an insight here.

*The **new middleman** will evolve further
into the **concierge**.*

Consequently, in markets where there are already
many business models of the **new middleman**,
it will become desirable to adopt
the strategy of **preemption**
aiming at evolving into
the **concierge** business model.

If so, what is this **concierge**?

It is a new extended **customer-centric** business model
that *goes beyond*
purchasing agent and **purchasing support**
to offer *services of*
lifestyle support and **lifestyle advice.**

In the online business, now
companies entering into this **new main battlefield**
have been increasing.

Chapter Three

When *Quantity* Exceeds a Specific Level, The *Quality* Changes Dramatically.

The Third Law

The Law of Development through
Transformation from Quantity to Quality.

When *quantity*
exceeds a specific level,
the *quality* changes dramatically.

As we discussed in the previous chapter,
by applying two laws of dialectic,
the law of development through **spiral process** and
the law of development through **negation of negation**,
we can foresee the **next main battlefield**.
We can foresee
where the **main battlefield** will move to.

However, when described in this way,
another question may arise in the reader's mind.

> *If so, when does the **main battlefield** shift?*

Put it another way,
in dialectic development, the questions are as follows:
> *When does the **revival** of nostalgic things occur?*
> *When does the **reversal** of current trends begin?*

Unfortunately, however, there is no method
for predicting clearly the period in which
this **shift of the main battlefield** will occur.
There is no method for **predicting** concretely
the period when
the main battlefield will shift.

But, there is a *method for judging*
the ***possibility*** of the shift occurring.

Actually, in dialectic,
there is one more **law** that teaches us this.
What is it?

It is
the law of development through
transformation from quantity to quality.

That is,

*When **quantity** exceeds a specific level,*
*the **quality** changes dramatically.*

That is the law.

If so, what is an example of this law?
The most familiar example
is the ***evaporation of water***.

When you put water in a kettle, and
apply heat from below, the temperature rises gradually.
And when the water temperature reaches 100 degrees,
the water changes to steam, bubbles form,
and **evaporation** begins.

This is a phenomenon by which,
when *the **quantity** called **water temperature***
increases, and exceeds 100 degrees,
*the **quality** changes from **liquid** to **gas***.

When *shares* exceed a specific level, a *de facto standard* naturally emerges.

Evaporation of water is an example in the natural world,
but there are many examples of this
also in society and markets.

For example,
when new products with different technical standards
generate intense competition in the market,
one of them occupies the dominant position in share,
and the shares exceed a specific level,
many customers, at an accelerated pace,
start buying the product.
And as a result the standard of that product
becomes the *de facto standard*
and it dominates the market.

This phenomenon also means that
*the increase in the **quantity** of this **share***
*brings about a change in its **quality**,*
*in the form of a **standard** or **monopoly**.*

In this way,
most things in the world have a property dictating that
*when their **quantity** exceeds a specific level,*
either instantly or rapidly,
*their **quality** will undergo a major change.*

This is because, behind the phenomena
called ***discontinuous change***, ***leap*** and ***evolution***,

238

exists the dialectic *law of transformation from quantity to quality*.

Let us discuss one more important example.
It is the case of the **new middleman** mentioned earlier.

When hearing about this discussion of
the new middleman,
the reader most likely harbors one question.

   Why has the new middleman appeared at this time?

That is the question.

The answer is clear.

The services called
purchasing agency and **purchasing support**
which the new middleman offers—
the customer needs for such services existed from the past.

This is *not the service of a **sales agency**
who promotes the sale of products
from the standpoint of the company,
but the service of a **purchasing agency**
who supports the purchase of products
from the standpoint of the customer.*

The customer needs for this service
have existed from the past.

Since long before the birth of the new middleman,
this is, *for customers, the most desirable service* and
a service which was in very strong demand.

But, it was extremely difficult to provide this service.

Why was that?

When there is a dramatic drop

in *cost*,

the *business model* evolves.

It is because *the **cost** was too high.*

That is, no matter how much
the service was needed by the customer,
the service of **purchasing agency** and **purchasing support**,
which the new middleman offers now,
cost too much to be realized.

Examples are the following services:
Gathering and offering information on every product
related to the special needs of the customer.
Acting all the procedure for the purchase
on behalf of the customer.

If we attempted to offer such service in business,
enormous costs would be incurred.
So, it was impossible to realize,
considering the cost burden to the customer.

That is, a great *cost barrier* existed.

This is the most important reason that
the new middleman did not appear in markets
despite the strong needs of the customer.

In other words, the excessive *communication costs*
to provide the information the customer needed
was the major reason why it would not work.

However, a **revolution** occurred.

*The Internet revolution broke down this **cost barrier**.*

This is because the Internet could cut
the **communication costs** for providing information
from company to customer
down to **1/1000th** of the cost before the Internet.
Actually, in the present age
after the broadband revolution and Web 2.0 revolution,
the cost has dramatically come down even more.

That is why the new middleman appeared.

By using websites and e-mail,
the **communication costs** to the customer
dropped dramatically.

For this reason, the service of
purchasing agency or **purchasing support**,
which had been impossible owing to excessive costs,
became possible to realize,
and many new middlemen appeared in markets.

If so, what does it mean?

*The **quantitative** change,*
which was the dramatic drop in
***communication costs**,*
*brought about a **qualitative** change,*
*which was the **evolution from the old middleman***
***to the new middleman**.*

When *cost* drops dramatically,
the *consciousness of the consumer*
changes greatly.

This is the law of development through
transformation from quantity to quality.

Now, when considering
the ***time to shift the main battlefield*** in the market,
it is extremely useful to know this law.

When discerning changes in the market,
and foreseeing where the main battlefield will shift to,
it helps us understand
what indices *to focus on* and
what quantities *to pay attention to*.

For example, let us discuss the ***broadband revolution***
which came after the Internet revolution.

*How has this **broadband revolution**
changed the **quality** of the market?*
In order to consider this,
what ***indices*** should we pay attention to?

Many experts focused on the quantity of
distribution of digital content,
especially, the distribution of music and movies.
This focus was because many experts predicted that
as broadband becomes popular,
many people would be able to listen to music
and watch movies freely by using the Internet.

It was also because they predicted that
a great quantity of digital content must be distributed
in order to realize that.

Of course, owing to the broadband revolution,
the circulation of music and movies
has become very large in quantity.
However, the most important thing that
the broadband revolution has actually changed
is not this **circulation of digital content**.

If so, what is it?

It is the ***consciousness of peopl***e.

This is because the broadband revolution has realized
a ***dramatic drop in Internet connection fees***.

Through the broadband revolution,
continuous connection and ***unlimited access***
became possible.

For this reason, the people
who had been *using the Internet*
mindful of connection fees,
are now able to use the Internet as they wish,
without worrying about cost.

And this has changed
the **consciousness of people** greatly.

When the *consciousness of the consumer* changes greatly, the market evolves into a *customer-centric market*.

For example, when purchasing a product,
it has become a trend *to purchase*
by making thorough comparisons between products
by *accessing lots of information* easily
on the Internet.

Also, it has become a trend *to purchase products*
by listening to the opinions of friends or acquaintances
and *listening to the voices of other consumers*
in the online community.

Thus the **consciousness of people** changed greatly.

That is, the services of **continuous connection**
and **unlimited access**, which were considered
to be **minor changes** in the broadband revolution,
fundamentally altered the consciousness of people
towards information.

This also is the law of development through
transformation from quantity to quality.

*The quantitative change in **Internet connection fees***
brought about a qualitative change in
*the **consciousness of people**.*

In this way, a curtain finally rose
when the **consciousness of people** changed
through this revolution.

*A full-fledged **customer-centric market**—*
the curtain has finally risen on this market.

The curtain of the **customer-centric market** has risen
not only because in the market
many **customer-centric business models** spread
and a number of **new middlemen** appeared.

*The curtain of the true **customer-centric market** finally rose*
*because the consciousness for **information** of*
the great number of customers and citizens
was fundamentally changed.

And, at that time,
the market began to enter the real stage of **evolution**.

That is, the **evolution of the market** does not mean simply
evolution of the **business model** or
evolution of the **middleman**.

It means the evolution of
*the **consciousness of the consumer** in the market*
and the evolution of
*the **consciousness of the people** in society.*

This is precisely what is meant by
the **evolution of the market** and the **evolution of society**.

By dramatically dropping *costs,*

we can accelerate

the *shift of the main battlefield.*

What is the law of development through
transformation from quantity to quality?
How do we implement this law strategically?

Up to this point, from these viewpoints,
we have discussed the following two items.

How do we foresee
*in what direction the **main battlefield** will shift,* and
*when will this **main battlefield** shift?*

However, one question will most likely arise
in the mind of the reader who hears such statements.

> *If so, how can we accelerate*
> *the shift of that **main battlefield**?*

Certainly, this is an important question.

If we are able to foresee in what direction
the **main battlefield** will move,
we can establish a strategic foothold
for **this battlefield** through preemption.
And we can wait for this main battlefield to come.
We have already discussed
the importance of the *strategy of preemption*.

However, if we adopt this **strategy of preemption,**
the next question we must face is
"how can we accelerate the shift of the main battlefield?"

For example, let us reflect on the above cases.
If, in the age of the broadband revolution,
we wanted to accelerate the arrival of
the **customer-centric market,**
what must we have done?

We must
spread the customer-centric business model or
foster new middlemen in markets.

These strategic measures are important,
but it is clear what the most important measure is.

We must *bring down communication fees.*

We need to accelerate this.
By doing this,
the **transformation from quantity to quality**
will necessarily occur.
And at some stage,
the consciousness of people towards information
will necessarily begin to change greatly.
And at that time,
the market will evolve into a **customer-centric market,**
not only at the level of
a **business model** or a **middleman,**
but also at the level of **market culture.**

That is, the effective strategy is to
*accelerate a qualitative change in **market culture** by*
*accelerating a quantitative change in **communication fees.***

By dramatically increasing

the *number of users,*

we can promote the *evolution of the market.*

In this way, in order to accelerate
the **transformation from quantity to quality**
in the market,
the *strategy of dropping the **price** of a product
below a specific level*
has become an important strategy.

And such a strategy of acceleration by
the **transformation from quantity to quality**
has actually been used sometimes in the past.

For example,
when promoting a new product in the market,
there are some cases where
the strategic objective of development and sales
is set to offer a product at an inexpensive price
which is lower than a specific price level.

It is well known that the popularity
was suddenly accelerated for products such as
DVD recorders and large screen TVs
*at the stage where the prices
dropped below a specific level.*

Consequently, when accelerating
the **transformation from quantity to quality**
in the market,

248

we sometimes need to *focus on the **quantity**, that is, the **price** of a product.*

However, in the age of the Internet revolution, in order to accelerate the evolution of the market, there is one other important **quantity** that we need to focus on.

What is that?

It is the ***number of users***.

In order to accelerate the **evolution of the market** in the age of the Internet revolution, not only the **price** of a product, but also the index called the **number of users** becomes extremely important.

If we consider the essence of the network society, this is only natural.

For example, telephones became convenient because many people owned them. If only a single individual owned a telephone, it would have no value. And, even if only a few people had them, the range of their utility would be limited. This is as true with the fax as with e-mail.

In this way, most of the technologies, products and services in a network society are useful because **they are used by many people**. This is called the ***network effect***.

When the number of users
exceeds a specific level,
self-acceleration begins.

Conversely,
the technologies, products, and services
in a network society
become useful to everyone,
as the number of people who use them increases.
So, more and more people
will begin to use them.

This means, in the words of the leading edge science,
namely the **science of complex systems**,
that *the technologies, products and services*
in the network society
now have the property of **self-acceleration**.
And for this reason, in the network society,
the **number of users** is an important index.

When the **number of users** increases
and exceeds a specific level,
at that point, **self-acceleration** begins
and the nature of society and markets begins
to change rapidly and on a large scale.

A well-known example
in which this fact was used strategically
is the strategy taken by **Netscape Communications, Inc.**
at the beginning of the Internet revolution.

By spreading the revolutionary software,
Netscape Navigator, Netscape took the initiative
to raise the curtain of the Internet revolution.
At the beginning it adopted the *strategy of
distributing the software free of charge to everyone.*
It was a strategy based on the idea that
the more the **number of users** increases,
the greater the value of the Internet browser becomes.

This strategy of **free distribution**,
which is called *freemium strategy* as well,
later brought about the success of many products
and it is no longer very unusual.
If we survey the world around us,
we will find many businesses in which
markets suddenly launch and develop
as the **number of users** exceed a specific level.

For example, in the 2000s
we saw a rapid expansion of *blogs.*
Since it is attractive for bloggers
to connect with each other
through track back and commenting,
the more the number of users increased,
the greater the merits became.
So, at a certain stage, they expanded explosively.

Consequently,
the strategy to rapidly increase the **number of users**
by venturing to implement
the free distribution of products
is also a *strategy for accelerating
the shift of the **main battlefield***
and an effective measure for accelerating
the **transformation from quantity to quality**.

The transformation from *quantity* to *quality* begins when *buzzwords* are forgotten.

Now, how can we judge *whether or not a **quantity** has exceeded a specific level as an index*?

There is no absolute method for this,
but there is one **indicator** which can be of some help.

The **indicator** is
*whether or not a **buzzword**
has been forgotten.*

Let us discuss a familiar example.
There are such items as the **telephone**, the **fax**,
the **Internet** and **e-mail**.
At the time when these new technologies,
products and services in the network societies
first emerge on the scene and expand throughout society,
these **buzzwords** attract attention and appear with great
frequency in the mass media.

However, *after they had spread throughout society
as a whole and penetrated it,
these **buzzwords** actually began to disappear.*

For example, in the past when the Internet revolution
had just begun,
the word **Internet** frequently appeared in the mass media,
and many people used it as a cool, cutting-edge **buzzword**.

However, now that the Internet has spread and penetrated
into all corners of society,
people who use smartphones to
get information from the web, for example,
are no longer consciously thinking
"well I guess I will use the Internet
to get some information."
They have even forgotten that they are using
the Internet terminals for that purpose.

That is, when we begin to forget that the technologies,
products and services are close at hand,
they have, in fact, adequately spread
throughout society and have penetrated it

For example, let us think about the **hybrid automobile**,
which is now popular as an environment-friendly car.
As long as people are conscious of the fact
that **they are driving a hybrid car**,
we cannot say that it has reached
its substantial popularity.
We can say that only after
it has faded from the consciousness of the people.

Consequently,
whether or not the **buzzword** has been forgotten
is one **indicator**.

It is only when it **has been forgotten**
that an important thing has really begun to happen.

The *transformation from quantity to quality*
has begun to happen quietly and profoundly in society.

Chapter Four

Things Which Oppose and Compete with Each Other Come to Resemble Each Other.

The Fourth Law

The Law of Development through
Interpenetration of Opposing Objects.

Things which oppose and compete with each other come to resemble each other.

Now, when gaining an insight into
the essence of changes in the world
and foreseeing the future,
there is one other important law in dialectic,
in addition to the following laws:

The law of development through **spiral process**.
The law of development through **negation of negation**.
The law of development through
transformation from quantity to quality.

The other important law is
the *law of development through*
***interpenetration of opposing object*s**.

That is,

*Things which oppose and compete with each other
come to resemble each other.*

That is the law.

Let us discuss this law in terms of
two laws we have already described.

Firstly, the *law of development through **spiral process***
is the law in which
old things are revived as if climbing a spiral staircase.
From another viewpoint, this means that
old things are revived with involving new things
and new things develop with involving old things.

Secondly,
the *law of development through **negation of negation***
is the law in which things once negated
return to their origins through being negated again.
From another viewpoint, it means that
new things that negate old things
return with old things negated.

That is,
***revival** in dialectic is*
*the **revival** including new things, and*
***negation** in dialectic*
*is the **negation** including the things negated.*

In other words, in dialectic, *two things*
which appear to oppose and compete with each other,
in a sense, *become included with each other,*
and as a result,
*both of them **merge** and become **integrated**.*

That is the law of development through
interpenetration of opposing objects.

Real business and

Internet business

will necessarily merge.

Let us take a concrete example.

At the beginning of the Internet revolution
the phrase *Real versus Internet* was often used.

This was a debate over which type of business was
superior, and advantageous in competition
between the *Real businesses* on the street and
the *Internet businesses* having shops online.

But, these phrases were soon replaced by
the phrase *click and mortar*.

That is, people started to recognize that
it was important in businesses
to combine successfully the Internet business of **click**
and the Real business of **mortar** and
to develop them strategically.

However, at present, phrases like
Real versus Internet and **click and mortar**
are no longer used.

This is because, *in all businesses*
the Real businesses and the Internet businesses
*have **merged** and* **integrated** *with each other.*

These days, there is no **Real** business
without considering using the **Internet**.

At present, many companies and shops
have their own websites and homepages on the Internet
in addition to their real shops.
And they are in the practice of taking orders
through their websites and e-mail.

On the other hand, now there is no **Internet** business
without considering having **Real** operations.
At the beginning of the Internet revolution,
during the Christmas rush in the US,
many Internet businesses that were selling products
faced the problem of late delivery,
and they were greatly criticized for this.
Today, naturally the Internet businesses are facing
the necessity to consider carefully combining
Real operations such as services of shop inventory control,
delivery service, telephone communications
and in-store product explanations.

In this way, the Real business and the early Internet business
were described as opposing each other,
symbolized by the phrase **Real versus Internet**.
Now, however, these businesses have *learned
from each other*, have undergone *interpenetration*,
and the business model that has *merged* the two
has become both common practice and mainstream.

Thus, there are a large number of examples of
development through
interpenetration of opposing objects
in many areas of business.

Brokerage firms and *banks* mutually evolve into *universal banks*.

For example, let us consider the *interpenetration of conventional brokerages and online brokerages*.
This is what is happening in the Japanese markets.

When the online brokerages first appeared on the scene,
the conventional brokerages believed
that **customers would not trade in
their important stocks by using the Internet**.
But they were overwhelmed by
the rapid growth of online brokerages,
and as a result they rapidly started to provide
online trading services.

However, it is interesting that on the other hand,
online brokerages that had once rejected real shops
have been opening actual shops on the street
in order to enhance their points of contact with customers.
That is, they have started in-store services.

And, as a result of this interpenetration taking place,
at present, every brokerage
is becoming an *evolved brokerage*
which offers general services
through the merging of the online and real shops.

Similarly, in the banking world
online banks appeared
which offer services on the Internet
without having physical locations.
And interpenetration occurred here also
through competition with *conventional banks*.
So at present, all banks have become ***evolved banks***
by integrating the online and real services.

Moreover, if we view this trend in the financial world
on a wider perspective, these brokerage firms
and banks are also undergoing interpenetration.

This interpenetration will occur as follows.
*Brokerage firms concentrating on **direct financing***
and *banks concentrating on **indirect financing***
were competing with each other and fighting
over customers in the field of financial services.
But through relaxation of regulations and liberalization
in the financial industry called the ***financial Big Bang***,
banks have moved into brokerage services, and
brokerage firms have moved into banking.
In this way, interpenetration has occurred.

As a result of such interpenetration, after all,
both brokerage firms and banks
are evolving in the direction of
general financial services called ***universal banks***.

This has already occurred in the financial industries
in Europe and the US,
and has been occurring in Japan as well.

For-profit companies and *non-profit organizations*

mutually

evolve into *social enterprises*.

However, such **interpenetration**
does not only occur within one industry, or
between different industries.
It happens also on a much larger scale.

For example, interpenetration occurs also between
for-profit companies and non-profit organizations.

This is because now two major trends
are emerging in the world.

The first is a trend towards
corporate social responsibility (CSR) *and*
sustainable development goals (SDGs).

That is, entering the 21st century,
social responsibility *and* **social contributions**
are now being demanded of *for-profit companies*,
which had tended to consider their main mission
to be the pursuit of profit.
That is, they have been expected to act
not only for the profit of their own companies,
but also for the benefit of society and
the future of humanity.

The second is a trend towards
social entrepreneur *and* **social business**.

For example,
non-profit organizations that have been conventionally
operated depending on benefactors' contributions and
government supports have been expected to adopt a style of
social entrepreneur and **social business**, which
would raise their operating revenue properly through
entrepreneurial spirit and entrepreneurial methods,
thus securing the independence and
sustainability of their operations.

This is, in a sense, the **interpenetration** that
the for-profit companies learned from the non-profits
concerning **social contribution**, *and*
the non-profit organizations learned from the for-profits
concerning **economic foundation**.

Consequently, in the coming age,
these two major trends of **CSR** and **SDGs**
as well as **social entrepreneur** and **social business**
will merge together.
As a result, a new form of business organization
called a **social enterprise**, which goes beyond
the two opposing terms **for-profit** and **non-profit**,
will appear.

In other words, this is a new form of business organization
which proclaims a clear objective of *making contributions*
to society through its main businesses,
and at the same time secures the *profits for*
the sustainability and development of the organization.

In the near future, many for-profit companies and
non-profit organizations will very likely
evolve into this new form of business organization.

Capitalism and *socialism*

have evolved

through interpenetration.

This example of **interpenetration**
exists not only in the economic world,
but also in the *political world*.

For example, under *two-party political institutions*,
this interpenetration often takes place.

Because, under a two-party system,
opposing parties are strongly conscious of
the demands of the electorate and try to incorporate
the good parts of the policies of their opponents,
and as a result their policies end up
being not too different from each other.

For this kind of ***interpenetration*** *of policies*,
as symbolized by policy changes in
the Conservative and Labour Parties in the UK,
there are many other cases around the world.

And, such **interpenetration**
also occurs in the *states* and in *social systems*.

In the past there was an age in which
the ***capitalist states*** of the US and Western Europe
and the ***socialist states*** of the USSR, Eastern Europe,
and China were opposing and in conflict with each other
as two social systems.

However, most of the **capitalist states**,
in the form of ***principles of social democracy***,
adopted policies for fulfilling social welfare
and improving the rights of the workers.

In contrast, the former **socialist states** of
Russia and China adopted
capitalism and market principles into their state system.

These are also examples of **interpenetration**
at the levels of states and social systems
that happened in the course of history.

In this way,
the dialectic law of development through
interpenetration of opposing objects
gives precious hints for gaining insight into
the essence of what is currently taking place
in companies, markets, and societies,
foreseeing what will happen,
and determining new policies and strategies.

Things which oppose and compete with each other
come to resemble each other.

If we look around,
there are numerous examples of this law,
from cases of products, personnel, and companies,
to cases of markets, economies and societies,
and from everyday events to historical events.

Chapter Five

Contradiction is the Driving Force
For the Development of the World.

The Fifth Law

The Law of Development through
Sublation of Contradiction.

Contradiction

is the driving force

for the development of the world.

So far, we have discussed
the following four laws of dialectic from the viewpoint of
how we can foresee the future:

The law of development through **spiral process**.
The law of development through **negation of negation**.
The law of development through
transformation from quantity to quality.
The law of development through
interpenetration of opposing objects.

However, at the root of these four laws,
exists the most fundamental law.

Now, let us discuss this fundamental law.
What kind of law is it?

It is
the law of development through
sublation of contradiction.

That is,

Contradiction *is the driving force*
for the development of the world.

That is the law.

To put it simply, this law means that:

All things contain within themselves **contradictions**,
but those very *contradictions* become
the *driving forces* *of their development.*
When such **contradictions** are not
resolved mechanically
but *sublated* *dialectically,*
their development is achieved.

In a sense,
this is the most important law underlying dialectic.
And this law represents the most basic idea of dialectic.

That is, things in the world change, develop, and evolve
because **contradictions** exist in those things.

And those very **contradictions** are
the **driving forces** of their development
and are none other than the *life forces* that
cause things to change, develop, and evolve.

This is the idea underlying dialectic.

And for this reason,
dialectic is called the *philosophy of contradiction*.

The essence of

management is

the *management of contradiction.*

Let us consider a concrete example.

The *contradiction between*
pursuit of profit *and* ***social contribution***
in managing a company—
when involved in managing a company,
what we often confront is
the contradiction between these two.

It is often said in Japan that *no one can live on air*.
So, as long as we are managing a company,
we must make a **profit** day by day.
And if not,
we can neither pay employees their salaries nor
continue to exist as a company.

However, on the other hand, it is also said that
man shall not live by bread alone.
People who happen to come together in a company
devote their lives to this company.
If so,
simply **paying employees their salaries**
is not the sole objective of the company.

To become a company where employees can feel
job satisfaction and the joy of working—
it is also an important goal for the company.
To this end,
it is important to value highly
the *social contributions* of the company.

However, **pursuit of profit** and **social contribution**
often appear as a **contradiction**
in the management scene.

For example, *price* symbolizes this contradiction.

If a company sells a product at a low price,
the customers will be happy
and it will be able to make a contribution to society.
But, as a result, profits of the company may diminish.
Conversely,
if it takes advantage of the monopolized market,
and sells at a high price, it may gain a large profit.
But sometimes the company will end up being criticized
as an *antisocial business*.

However, excellent companies have
an admirable way of coping with such a **contradiction**.

The *management of contradiction* is it.

The companies practice it in an excellent way.

If so, what kind of management is this?

The *management of contradiction*

is management through

the *sublation* of contradiction.

No dichotomic judgment is it.

That is
the point of the **management of contradiction**.

This is because if we mechanically
*make a **dichotomic judgment***
to cope with a **contradiction**,
the *life force will be lost*.

For example, if we make the dichotomic judgment that
for a company, pursuit of profit is everything,
we may realize an increase in
the performance of the company for a short period,
but people will perceive the **company as having
no good will** and its reputation will be diminished.
And, along with this,
the employees will lose their motivation for working,
and in the long view, both the productivity and
creativity of the company will be lessened and lost.

However, on the other hand,
if we make a dichotomic judgment that
for a company, social contribution is everything,
we will lose sight of our foundation.
Consequently, profits will not go up,
the company cannot continue,
and it will be unable to realize its ideal.

272

As mentioned above, for the company,
the existence of a **contradiction** is, in a sense,
exactly what generates the **life force** of the company.

Consequently, if a company resolves the **contradiction**
through a mechanical **dichotomic judgment**,
it will lose not only the **contradiction**
but also its **life force** and its **driving force**.
Then both progress and development
will stop right there.

And this is a **principle** that applies to everything,
including markets and society,
not only to companies.

So, what should we do?
If we do not make such a **dichotomic judgment**,
what should we do?

We should apply the ***sublation*** *of dialectic.*

Now then, what does **sublation** mean?

This is a German term, ***aufheben***.
It refers to a *process by which two things that*
appear to mutually contradict and oppose each other
are elevated to a higher dimension
by affirming, including, integrating and transcending
them without negating one or the other.

Let us discuss this with a concrete example.

The point of the *management of contradiction* is to strike a balance by swinging the pendulum.

Let us consider the example of
the contradiction we described earlier
concerning **pursuit of profit**
and **social contribution** in a company.

To **sublate** the contradiction between these two means
to not make a **dichotomic judgment** by negating either
pursuit of profit or **social contribution**
while affirming the other,
but to affirm, include and integrate both of them.
And, by achieving this,
we can create an excellent company.

For example, the following *three phrases* that
have always been used in the management world of Japan
represent this **sublation** exactly.

*"The company first contributes
to society through its main business."*

"Profits are proof of contributing to society."

*"The fact that a large profit has been
given to the company
represents a call of the people to use this profit
to make further contributions to society."*

These phrases from **Japanese style management**
deeply represent the *management philosophy*,
which means to not consider **pursuit of profit**
and **social contributions** as two oppositions,
even if they appear to be mutually contradictory,
but to ***sublate*** *the contradicti*on between the two.

Now, if we do not take the viewpoint of
resolution of contradiction,
but take the viewpoint of
sublation of contradiction,
how should executives and managers
in the actual workplace pursue correctly
such a management style?
If we should not negate mechanically
one of the two which **contradicts** the other,
then *how should we practice*
*this **management of contradiction**?*

Let me state it plainly.

*We should swing the **pendulum**.*

That is, as if a **pendulum** is swinging
back and forth between two end points,
we should *push the **pendulum** between*
the two things which oppose and contradict each other.
In this way, we should *strike a balance between them*.

When management becomes one sided,
we swing the **pendulum** in the opposite direction
to bring about an overall balance.

The *management of contradiction* is needed not only in corporate management but also in public administration and politics.

For example, let us consider a **contradiction**
that is often discussed within companies:

Short-term profits *versus **long-term strategies**.*

The **pendulum** is needed for this as well.

For example, when the organization as a whole
emphasizes the securing of **short-term profits** so greatly
that they think only of the immediate tasks and
lose sight of the future vision,
executives and managers will venture to insist on
the importance of **long-term strategies**.

Conversely, when the organization as a whole
emphasizes the importance of **long-term strategies**
so greatly that they think only of the future vision and
lose sight of the immediate tasks,
executives and managers will rigorously insist on
the importance of **short term profits**.

The **management of contradiction**
that executives and managers need to *practice
means precisely to **strike a balance** between
the management tasks viewed as **contradictions**.*
It also means to continue to swing the **pendulum**
perceiving sensitively the condition of the organization
in order to strike such a balance.

And by continuing to swing the pendulum
and striking a balance,
executives and managers *promote both*
*the **learning** of each individual member of the organization*
*and the **learning** of the organization as a whole.*

Under what conditions or in what situations
should they focus on **short-term profits**
or put emphasis on **long-term strategies**?

Executives and managers must continue
to boldly swing the pendulum
in order that each individual member of the organization
may learn the issues above
to the level of ***spontaneous judgment***
and the organization as a whole may learn those issues
*to the level of **corporate culture**.*

And this way of swinging the pendulum
is not sufficient if viewed only from the overall
framework of the **company as a whole.**
Naturally, whether in the marketing division
or the development division,
the pendulum should be swung for *each **division***
to strike a different balance.
Sometimes it is necessary to swing the pendulum
for a different balance adjusting to the personality and
the character of *each **individual employee**.*

However, in order to practice
this **management of contradiction**,
executives and managers, in fact, must have
multiple personality within themselves.
The meaning of this will be discussed in detail
in Chapter Six.

The essence of administration is
to strike a balance between
market principles and *government regulations.*

And this **management of contradiction**
is not only required of business management.
It is also required of *administration and politics*.

For example, let us consider the *contradiction*
between **market principles** *and* **government regulations**
in government policy.
The **management of contradiction** of these two is
needed for both politicians and administrators.

That is, the following questions can be raised
concerning services that are to be offered in a society:
To what extent should we entrust such services to
the private sector and market principles?
To what extent should we expect the government to bear
and treat these services as objects of regulations?

The issue of the optimum balance between
market principles and **government regulations**
is fundamental for policy making,
and is an issue in *state management* required of
politicians and administrators.

And up until now,
in many capitalist sates including Japan,
the introduction of **market principles** and
the realization of **small government** has
become a major political challenge.

278

The **pendulum** has been swinging strongly
in the direction of **market principles**.

However, if we look at this from a long-term viewpoint,
politicians and administrators must return the swing of
the **pendulum** at an appropriate point in time
to strike a balance in policy
by recognizing the conditions of the period.

Consequently, the **pendulum** has been moving
in the direction of **market principles** up until now,
so naturally, at some appropriate point in the future,
it will need to swing back
in the direction of **government regulations**.

Another example is the *contradiction in politics between*
self-responsibility and *relief for the weak*.

In countries such as Japan, which have practiced
a policy of **government regulations** and **big government**
for a long period of time, the people are penetrated with
the *consciousness of dependence*:
If I am in trouble, the government would be of help.
But, as large negative influences of such an attitude
come to be pointed out, the **pendulum** today is swinging
in the direction of **self-responsibility** and **self-help**.

However, from a long-term viewpoint,
necessarily, at some point,
the **pendulum** will again swing in the direction of
relief for the weak for people who have suffered from
competitions, and people who need aid in an aged society.

But, the *most important thing in this **management of***
***contradiction** is the judgment of timing:*
At what point in time should the pendulum be swung back?

We must not forget the importance of this fact.

With *contradiction* becoming a life force,

the world

will change, develop and evolve.

In this way, **management of contradiction** is
the act of ***sublating*** *the contradiction* between
two opposing senses of value by continuing to swing
the **pendulum** between the two,
which means, in the *short term*,
to strike an ***overall balance*** that is optimal
for the current condition, and in the *long term*,
to realize the growing of the individual,
the learning of the organizations,
and the maturing of society.

This is the basic method of **management of contradiction**,
which is how to cope with the **contradictions**
in society, markets and organizations
based on the law of
development through **sublation of contradiction**.

And we have already discussed
the idea of dialectic which
lies at the roots of this **management of contradiction**.

Contradiction *is the driving force*
for the development of the world.

That is, in order to gain an insight into
the basic nature of things in this world,
foresee their future, and formulate policies and strategies,
it is important to first look deeply into
the **contradictions** in front of us that are inherent
in society, markets and organizations.

And it is also important to consider carefully
what will happen in the future
in society, markets and organizations
with this **contradiction** becoming the driving force.

We should remember the following fact.

*The world in which we live
is filled with **contradictions**.*

And, ***contradictions*** *are*
*the **driving forces** of the development of the world*
*and the **life forces** of the world.*
Therefore, the world in which we live
will change, develop, and evolve.

For this reason, we should not mechanically
negate these **contradictions**.

We must *dialectically*
sublate *these* **contradictions**.

The *capacity of a person*
is none other than the *power of soul*
that can embrace great contradictions.

Now then, in society, markets and organizations,
what is the *important wisdom*
required of politicians, administrators and executives
in order to cope with these **contradictions**
and in order to sublate these **contradictions**?

The noted Buddhist Katsuichiro Kamei
said the following important words:

Dichotomic judgment *is a weakness of soul.*

Certainly, as these words suggest,
we sometimes tend to make **dichotomic judgments**
when we are confronted with various **contradictions**, and
find ourselves in distress and confusion.

"First, economic growth is everything."
"There is no help for it, if the weak are selected out."
"Business, after all, is all about making profits."

We tend to escape into such **dichotomic judgments**.

282

However, what is essentially required of
such persons as the leaders of society, including
politicians, administrators and executives,
is to *continue to struggle with*
the **contradictions** *in front of them*
without escaping from these **contradictions**.

In other words, what is needed for them in the face of
the various **contradictions** existing in this society is
to confront them,
to hold them in the core of their minds,
and to continue struggling with them
to find a way to sublate these **contradictions**
without making **dichotomic judgments**.

This struggle demands a capability
which may be called ***strength of the soul***.

However, when we understand the importance of this,
we will find the true meaning of the words which
from the past have been bestowed upon
outstanding leaders in politics and management.

A person of great capacity is it.

This refers to a *person who can embrace in their mind*
great **contradictions***, confront them,*
and continue to struggle with them.

This is the kind of person
that these words would be bestowed upon.

When we acquire *dialectic thinking*, we also acquire the *ability of dialogue* to gain insight into essence through dialogue.

Now, in order to carry out **management of contradiction**,
what kind of *ability* is required
for such leaders as
politicians, administrators, and executives?

Let me state it simply.

It is the *ability of dialectic dialogue*.

Let me state it another way.

Just through dialogue,
our thinking naturally becomes deeper.
And the essence of things becomes apparent.

That is the kind of ability required.

And, actually, by understanding **dialectic**,
this ability will be naturally acquired.
Because, as the word **dialectic** itself suggests,
it was born in the age of ancient Greece
as a *technique of dialogue*.

The one who used this **dialectic** was **Socrates**,
a philosopher well known from *Apology*, written by Plato.

Socrates valued *dialectic* highly
as a technique for seeking the truth.
He used *dialectic* as a *technique*
to deepen thinking and
to arrive at the truth through **dialogue**.

However, this **dialectic**
is a technique totally different from
debate or **discussion**.

Debate, literally, is a technique in which people
holding different opinions argue with each other and
attempt to prove one's own argument is correct.

And, *discussion* is a technique in which people
holding different opinions gather and
learn various viewpoints from each other
by exchanging their opinions.

In contrast to the above, **dialectic** is a technique
in which people holding opposing opinions
move into deeper thinking through dialogue.
In other words,
this is not a **technique for engaging in an argument**,
but a *technique for deepening thinking*.

If so, what is this technique, specifically?

Thinking becomes deeper
through the process of
thesis, *antithesis*, and *synthesis*.

This is the *deepening of thinking through*
thesis, antithesis, and synthesis.

That is, dialectic is
a technique by which people deepen thinking through
the process of **thesis**, **antithesis**, and **synthesis**.

To put it simply, it is a technique by which
one person states an opinion (thesis) and
another person states an opposing opinion (antithesis),
and through a dialogue based on each opinion,
both of them arrive at
a deeper understanding (synthesis) by including, integrating
and sublating the two opposing opinions.

Let us discuss this concretely.

For example, concerning issues in child education,
one person says, *"in education, kindness is essential."*
In response to this, another person says,
"no, in education strictness is essential."

At this stage, their opinions are completely
in opposition and in contradiction with each other.
If the two of them engage in earnest dialogue,
their understanding will deepen further.

For example,
opinions will be offered such as:
"I wonder if not scolding a child means true kindness?"
Or *"maybe, occasionally scolding a child strictly could be
real kindness."*

Also, on the other hand, opinions will be offered such as:
*"behind strictness,
there must be no anger in the scolding person"*; or
*"in the depths of strictness, there must be a heart
which believes deeply in the potential of the child."*

And then, in the midst of exchanging such opinions,
the thinking of both people is deepened,
and the true meaning of the notions of
kindness and strictness
in child education becomes clear.

Ultimately, eyes will be opened to
*a deeper level of education which is
neither simply kind
nor simply strict, but includes, integrates
and sublates both kindness and strictness.*

This is **dialectic** as a **technique of dialogue**.

Dialogue

is a technique of wisdom

which surpasses *debate* and *discussion*.

As mentioned above, this dialectic is
neither *debate* in which we simply engage in
a clash of opinions
nor *discussion* in which we simply exchange opinions
but an extremely creative technique of *dialogue*
in the sense that we can deepen each other's thinking.

Consequently,
in our daily **discussion**,
if we apply the technique of **dialectic dialogue**,
our discussions will necessarily become creative ones.

However, the current trends in the world today are
the technique of **debate**, which is
how to argue down opponents with speaking skills, and
the technique of *logical thinking*, which is
how to reach a logically correct conclusion.

Of course, these techniques have
their own value and role,
but we must understand the existence of
the **technique of wisdom**,
which at a higher level
surpasses these techniques.

The technique of **debate** tends to end up being
unproductive, where people cannot humbly learn
from each other and move into deeper thinking
because debate is, in many cases, limited to situations
where people point out the faults of
the opinions of their opponents and insist on
the superiority of their own opinions over the other.

On the other hand,
since the technique of *logical thinking* basically
emphasizes logical consistency
and eliminates contradictions.
It *does not have the viewpoint of sublating* **contradiction**
which is a driving force and a life force of
the development of things.
For this reason, this technique is useful to some degree
in solving simple problems, but is not very useful
as a **technique of wisdom** for considering
difficult problems in depth and
asking a question that has no answer.

Therefore, if we acquire
the techniques of **debate** and **logical thinking**,
we should advance and acquire the techniques of
dialectic dialogue and *dialectic thinking*.

This is because,
when we acquire this **technique of wisdom** called dialectic,
for the first time before us will rise
a curtain on a wonderful **world of wisdom**.

And then, we will be able to
deepen our thinking through dialogue,
gain an insight into the essence of things,
and foresee the future.

Chapter Six

The Future Forseen by Dialectic Thinking.

12 Paradigm Shifts That Will Happen
In the Future of Human Society.

When the world achieves *dialectic development,*
a *paradigm shift* will occur
in the worldview and the value system.

Up to this point, in Chapters One through Five,
we have discussed
the *Five Laws* of *dialectic*:

The law of development through **spiral process**;

The law of development through **negation of negation**;

The law of development through
transformation from quantity to quality;

The law of development through
interpenetration of opposing objects; *and*

The law of development through **sublation of contradiction**.

These are the **Five Laws**.

And we have discussed that
many different things in this world,
ranging from products and services
to markets and economies, as well as societies and cultures,
are changed, developed and evolved
based on these **Five Laws**.

Now then, if we deeply understand these **Five Laws**
and *foresee the future by applying the laws,*
what kind of future will appear to us?

292

We shall discuss these issues in this chapter.

However, before this,
we must understand one important thing.
That is **what** *we should pay attention to*
when we foresee the future.

Let me state this in one word.

It is the ***paradigm***.

In foreseeing change, development and evolution
in the world,
it is important to
watch from the viewpoint of
what kind of ***paradigm shift*** will occur.

This is because both substantial changes and
important changes in the world are always
accompanied by a *fundamental shift*
in the ***basic worldview and basic value system***,
namely a ***paradigm***.

Consequently, in this chapter, we will discuss and foresee
by applying these **Five Laws** of dialectic,
*what kind of **paradigm** shift will occur*
in various fields in the world, and
as a result what kind of **future** will come.

Let us briefly describe this future.

The voluntary economy
will merge with the monetary economy
and a *new economic principle* will emerge.

What we should first foresee is
the *paradigm shift in* **economies**.

What will happen in the field of **economies** in the future?

We have already discussed this in Chapter One.

*The **voluntary economy** will be revived.*

That is,
the **voluntary economy**, which is an *economic activity*
created by people seeking the **satisfaction of mind**
based on goodwill and affection,
will be revived as a mainstream economic activity in society
and increase its influence.

And it will increase its influence on society relative to
the **monetary economy**, which is an *economic activity*
created by people seeking the **acquisition of money**
and has been the mainstream in capitalist societies
up to now.

Now, why will this happen?

We can foresee this from the law of development
through **spiral process**.

Namely, the *gift economy* that was
the oldest economic principle for humanity—
*this **old nostalgic economic principle** will be revived,*
based on the law of spiral development,
*accompanied by **new values**.*

If so, what will happen after this **revival**?

*The **voluntary economy** and the **monetary economy***
will merge together.

And then, a *new economic principle* will emerge.

This can also be easily foreseen by a dialectic law.
It is the *law of development through*
***interpenetration of opposing objects**.*

That is, **things which oppose and compete with
each other come to resemble each other**.
As stated by this law,
these two economic principles will interpenetrate,
and will merge into one economic principle.

And, in fact, this is no longer merely something **foreseen**.
It has already become a **real** trend.

Why is this?

It is because the *Web 2.0 revolution* has occurred.

The **Web 2.0 revolution**
as the second stage in the **Internet revolution**—
this **evolved Internet revolution**
has already produced many concrete cases
for this new economic principle.

Business models

will be expanding to

social systems.

For example, let us consider **amazon.com**.

The business model of this site has already
brought about very high profits.
It is an excellent business model
representing the *monetary economy*.

Now then, on this site,
what kind of service is enjoying
the greatest popularity among users?

It is the information service of **product review**.

This is a very useful service for users
who are planning to purchase books,
and it has greatly increased
the value of amazon.com.

However, these **product reviews** are
not written by amazon.
These **review comments** are **grassroots comments**
that are written spontaneously and without compensation
by the people using this site themselves.

In fact, this service is produced by the *voluntary economy*.

The amazon **business model** is, in fact,
what should be called a *social system based on*
a totally new economic principle that is a merging of
the **monetary economy** *and the* **voluntary economy**.

And this merging has not only occurred in amazon.
Grassroots video sites such as **YouTube**,
grassroots photo sites such as **Flickr**,
all of these business models that use
so-called *UGC (User Generated Content)*
are social systems based on
this **new economic principle**.
And, in this sense, **Google**, which is
the largest online business at the present time, is
essentially a business model that uses UGC
made public through worldwide sites and blogs.
It is, after all, a social system based on
this **new economic principle**.

Now, what about **Linux** which is regarded as
a representative of the **voluntary economy**?
This also actually achieved a merging with
the **monetary economy**.
The reason is as follows:
Linux itself is a software that has been developed by
many software engineers gathering voluntarily from
all over the world and contributing their efforts
without compensation, but through offering various
services to companies that introduce Linux,
the business models of many IT companies
have been created.

Now then, is the merging of
the **monetary economy** and the **voluntary economy**
a movement only in the world of the Web 2.0 revolution?

Not at all.

The trends of *SDGs* and *social business* will lead in the merging of voluntary economy and monetary economy.

Now, if we take a broad view of society,
great trends have developed in the direction of
the merging of these two,
both from the **monetary economy** side
and from the **voluntary economy** side.
These are the two trends that we discussed in Chapter One.

One is a trend of
corporate social responsibility (CSR) *and*
sustainable development goals (SDGs).

This is a trend which demands
social responsibility of **for-profit businesses**,
and moreover, requires
social contribution in the activities of companies.

In the midst of this worldwide trend of CSR and SDGs,
many companies are developing activities for social
contributions using part of their profits, and are
implementing policies to encourage
their employees as well to join volunteer activities.

This is, in a sense, a trend that
the **monetary economy** is incorporating
the **voluntary economy** into itself.

Another is a trend of
social entrepreneurship *and* **social business**.

This also has become a worldwide trend,
which has emerged to solve the problems
that conventional non-profit organizations,
foundations and volunteer organizations were faced with.

Conventionally, such **non-profit organizations**
have operated proclaiming **social contributions**.
But since they have operated relying on
benefactors' contributions and government support,
they have been faced with the fundamental problem that
they could not continue their activities
if those contributions and support were cut off.

And then, what has been born after reflecting on these
problems is **social entrepreneurship** and **social business**,
which adopt the management technique of entrepreneurship
in the operation of their organizations, create profits from
their own operations of social contribution, and thus
aim at securing the independence and sustainability of
their activities.

That is, this trend of **social entrepreneurship** and
social business is, in a sense, a trend indicating that
the **voluntary economy** is incorporating
the **monetary economy** into itself.

As symbolized by such examples as
the case of the **Web 2.0 revolution**,
the case of **CSR** and **SDGs**, and
the case of **social entrepreneurship** and **social business**,
in various fields of society today,
a **new economic principle** has been born
through the merging of the **monetary economy** and
the **voluntary economy**,
and now it is penetrating all corners of society.

In order to solve the global warming problem, the creation and application of a *new economic principle* are required.

In fact, it is of an extremely great significance that
this *new economic principle* is born in this age.

That is because this **new economic principle** is
a *highly useful solution for*
the global environmental problems, including
global warming, which confront the world now.

As a main *economic method to solve these problems*,
a method called **internalization of external economies**
has been adopted up until now.

To explain concretely, this method is as follows:

In modern society, various costs
including damage to health, social uneasiness,
environmental measures and environmental remediation
are generated by environmental pollution and destruction.
They are called *social costs* or *external diseconomies*,
and originally exist **externally** to the market economy.

To solve this problem of these external diseconomies,
by introducing environmental regulations
based on the ***polluter-pays principle***,
governments demand companies responsible for
environmental pollution to bear the costs of
environmental measures, environmental remediation and
compensation for health damage,

300

and to reflect them in the cost of their products and services.

By these methods,
social costs and **external diseconomies**
were incorporated into the market economy,
and environmental measures were promoted
through the market principle.
This method is called
internalization of external economies.

To state this in another way, *it is a method by which
the* **social costs** *and* **external diseconomies** *existing
outside of the* **monetary economy**
were incorporated into the **monetary economy**.

Of course, this is one extremely effective method, and
has been employed to solve the global warming problem
as the policy of **emissions trading**.
But actually, in the coming age, one other
economic method will become more important.

This is the method of applying a **new economic principle**
that is the merging of
the **monetary economy** and the **voluntary economy**.

In other words, it is a method for *aiming to solve
global environmental problems*
not by **internalizing** the voluntary economy existing
outside of the monetary economy
but *by* **merging** *these two economic principles*.

To put it concretely, it is a *technique for promoting
the solution of the global warming problem
by connecting business models of private companies
with the volunteer minds of grassroots consumers.*

Now then, what kind of technique is this?

Corporate currency and *local currency*

are accelerating

a new economic principle.

One example of this is a **carbon offset product**,
which is spreading rapidly around the world.

This kind of product is as follows:
A company promises to use a part of the selling price of
the product to reduce an amount of CO_2 equivalent to
what is emitted during the manufacturing of that product.

As concrete measures, various methods have been
suggested such as forestation, forest conservation,
investment in natural energy, direct capture of CO_2,
emissions trading, and so forth.
These products are, in one sense, *aimed at connecting*
the market needs of the consumer, which is the
people's wish to purchase products they want, *with*
the voluntary mind of the consumer, which is the
people's wish to conserve the global environment.
In other words, it is a new social system which is
created by the merging of the monetary economy
and the voluntary economy.

And, in the midst of this trend,
companies have appeared that *use* **corporate currency**
for global warming countermeasures
and global environment conservation.
Corporate currency means service points that
companies give to the purchasers of their products.

This is a system in which *consumers can ask a company*
*to use **corporate currency***
for conservation of the global environment,
instead of using it for their own sake.

Furthermore, this trend has brought about a new system
in which *consumers can contribute their own*
***corporate currency** to social entrepreneurs,*
NPOs and NGOs.
This trend will join together
with a worldwide trend of CSR and SDGs
and greatly promote the evolution of **corporate currency**
going forward.

Another example is ***local currency***.
This is, like corporate currency, a system that is
spreading in various localities around the world
to promote voluntary economy in each locality.
These trends of **local currency** and **corporate currency**
will also connect with each other and merge together
in order to promote the activation of the voluntary economy.

Now then, what will such trends of **corporate currency** and
local currency bring about moving forward?

It is *an evolution in the **consciousness** of people*
*towards **currency***.

That is, up to now, for many people in the world
currency was merely a ***means to satisfy their own desires***.
However, in the coming age,
many people will understand that
currency is a ***means to change society***,
so they will enhance their consciousness towards currency
and move towards various actions to enact such change.

Innovation itself will evolve from *beneficiary innovation* to *participatory innovation*.

Now, what is the next paradigm shift
that will occur in these trends?

It is a *paradigm shift in* **innovation**.

That is, in the near future,
spiral development and **regression to the origin**
will occur also in **innovation**.

If so, what kind of regression to the origin will occur?

*Many people will come to participate
in the process of innovation in society.*

Such regression to the origin will occur.

In past times, in communities of older societies,
the wisdom for improving the communities was
discussed freely and equally
among their members.

However, as modern times came along,
specialization has occurred.

That is, as specialist knowledge
for solving problems became sophisticated and
that specialist knowledge became
the exclusive domain of only a limited number of people,
naturally, **specialists** in various fields came into being.
And the wisdom of these small numbers of people
came to create innovations for changing
the community and the society in their respective fields.

However, in the coming age, many people
will come to participate in the innovation process again.

Now then, why will such regression to the origin occur?

This is also because
the *Web 2.0 revolution* has occurred.

In other words,
because through this revolution,
people have come to be able to access
most of the knowledge
necessary for solving their problems
in communities and societies on the Web.
And because, through the Web,
many people have come to be able to
offer their own knowledge and wisdom as well as
opinions and ideas to communities and societies.

That is, many people have come to be able to participate
in the innovation process in communities and societies.

The words which symbolize this
have begun to be expressed along with
the **Web 2.0 revolution**.

Through the *Web 2.0 revolution*
the age of *collective intelligence* and
wisdom of crowds has begun.

Open source.
Community solution.
Prosumer-based development.

These are the words going around.

Open source refers to the method
of finding solutions to problems by posing questions
broadly to society as a whole
and gathering knowledge and wisdom not only from
professional engineers in companies or
policy specialists in government,
but also from the general public at large in,
for example, the development of software such as Linux and
the planning of government policy.

Similarly, *community solution* refers to the method
of arriving at solutions by posing questions
in communities in which many people gather
and getting the members of the communities
to solve their problems
by exchanging their opinions and ideas
freely and voluntarily.

Prosumer-based development refers to the method,
advocated prophetically in 1980
by the futurist **Alvin Toffler**
in his work *The Third Wave*,
of developing new products through collaboration between
the *producer* and the *consumer*.

In this way, in the world after the **Web 2.0 revolution**,
a great paradigm shift has occurred.

From **beneficiary innovation**
to **participatory innovation**—
this paradigm shift has occurred.

Now, the paradigm shift has occurred
from **beneficiary innovation**, in which
a small number of specialists and researchers
create innovations while a large number of people
merely receive benefits from those innovations,
to **participatory innovation**, in which
a large number of people participate
in the process of innovation by offering
their own knowledge and wisdom.

That is, through the **Web 2.0 revolution**,
the *method of innovation itself*
has achieved innovation.
And the words symbolizing this innovation
are as follows:

Wisdom of crowds.
Collective intelligence.

A paradigm shift will occur
from *indirect democracy*
to *direct democracy*.

That is, in the coming age,
not only the knowledge of a small number of specialists,
but also the knowledge and wisdom of
a large number of people at the grassroots level,
will become driving forces
to solve the problems in society and change society.

This is what those two phrases,
wisdom of crowds and **collective intelligence**, mean.

And, this is the essence of
a paradigm shift from **beneficiary innovation**
to **participatory innovation**
brought about by the **Web 2.0 revolution**.

However, if we understand the essence of
this paradigm shift in **innovation**,
we should also understand that it will naturally
bring about another paradigm shift.

It is a *paradigm shift in **democracy***.

If so, what does the paradigm shift
in democracy mean?

From **indirect democracy**
to **direct democracy**—
this paradigm shift will occur.

But, when described in this way,
many readers will most likely think:

> In the field of politics,
> indirect democracy by the **representative system**
> will come to an end and **direct democracy** will begin,
> in which many people will participate in politics
> by using the Web.

Certainly, such a trend will occur.
It is a trend called ***digital democracy***.

However, what I want to state here is
not *democracy in the field of* ***politics***.

We unconsciously think of the term **democracy**
as a **political** term.
But that is by no means the case.

That is because, in the coming age,
both in the world of ***economy***
and in the world of ***culture***,
democracy *will be realized, and furthermore,*
direct democracy *will be realized.*

Why is this?

Direct democracy will spread
not only in the field of *politics*,
but also in the fields of *economy* and *culture*.

The reason for this
is the **participatory innovation** mentioned above.

Through the realization of this
participatory innovation,
direct democracy will be finally realized
both in the field of **economy** and in the field of **culture**.

Conversely, *up until now*
both in the field of **economy** *and*
in the field of **culture**,
various activities have been conducted through
indirect democracy *by the* **representative system**.

For example, for a particular product,
even though
the *needs of the consumers* were of great variety,
a company would study the customer needs
through *market surveys*, narrow down the specification
and design of the product, and produce it.
Consequently, consumers were forced to purchase
a **product that most closely met their own needs**
from a *limited variety of products*.

However, through the **Web 2.0 revolution** and
the subsequent **Web 3.0 revolution**,
this situation will change greatly.

310

The reason is as follows:

Through these revolutions,

prosumer-based development will further spread,

long tail marketing will grow more popular,

and ***high mix, low volume production***

will grow more common.

So, in the coming age, *consumers will be able to*

design, order, and purchase products that they want

as ***products made just for themselves.***

This means that

direct democracy *in economy* will be realized.

What will be realized going forward is

not conventional **representative, indirect democracy**,

in which a company bringing out products most close

to consumer needs would gain support of consumers,

but ***participatory, direct democracy***,

in which consumers directly express their needs and

purchase products realizing their needs.

And the same paradigm shift will occur

in the field of ***culture***.

For example, in the great trend of the culture of **music**,

a system has been adopted in which

a *major music label or music production company*

would discover star musicians, cultivate them,

promote them through massive advertisement

and create a great boom in the market.

However, this system will also be changed greatly

through the **Web 2.0/3.0 revolutions**.

Democracy will deepen
from the participation of people in *decision-making*
to the participation of people in *social change*.

This change will be caused by following two movements.

Firstly, unknown musicians have become *able to individually and freely produce their original songs, perform them and make them public through websites* without asking for the help of major music labels and music production companies.

Secondly, if their songs are so good as to arouse the empathy of the public, *in the world of the Web, their evaluation and reputation will spread rapidly among many people and the musicians* will be able to *create a new culture in the world of music.*

This is *a trend which will be born commonly in creative and artistic worlds,* not only in the world of music but also painting and photography, computer graphics and movies, as well as novels and poetry.

In other words, this means that, through the **Web 2.0 revolution**, an age has begun in which *even grassroots people can freely engage in the activity of creation and art to express themselves and freely make public their works to society.*

312

And if creation and art can be cultivated
both by the people who create and produce them
and by the people who appreciate and criticize them,
then, the **Web 2.0 revolution**
has opened the curtain on an age
in which grassroots people can participate on both sides.

To state it in another way,
direct democracy *will be realized*
not only in the world of politics and economy,
but also in the world of creation of culture.

However, this never means
that professional creators and artists,
superior viewers and critics will become unnecessary.

Just like the fact that
a high mountain always has a broad foot below it,
the *more people will participate in*
such a world of creation of culture,
the higher the standards of the professional
will become in the world.

In this way, if we understand
that **direct democracy** will be realized moving forward,
not only in the world of politics,
but also in the worlds of economy and culture,
then we have to understand *the most important ideas*
*in the depth of the word **democracy.***

Democracy does not simply mean that
many people participate in ***decision-making***.
Democracy does mean that
many people participate in ***social change***.

The age of

non-linguistic communication and

image communication has begun.

Let us discuss next a *paradigm shift in* **communication**.

Now, what will happen in the field of **communication**
going forward?

In this field as well, **spiral development** will occur.
As a result,
nostalgic communication will be revived.

What kind of communication will this be?

It will be *non-linguistic communication*.

That is, in the coming age,
communication that does not use **language** will spread.

This is obvious by looking at the world after
the **Web 2.0 revolution**.

For example, let us take **YouTube**, which is accessed by
an overwhelming number of people around the world.
On this site, an infinite number of grassroots videos are
uploaded, most of which are not messages expressed
in texts or words but *messages expressed in videos*.

Similarly, the grassroots photo site **Flickr**,
enjoying high popularity now, is a site
in which most of the uploaded content is not
messages expressed in texts or words but
non-linguistic messages expressed in photos.

Also, even in websites and blogs,
both delivering messages and expressing oneself
through photos, videos, music, and sound
are increasing rapidly.

What is happening here?

*The age of **image communication**—*
this has begun.

This is a *culture* in which
people convey their messages not through texts and words
but *through photos, videos, music and sound.*
That is, a *culture* in which people convey
their messages *through non-linguistic information
and image information* has been spreading.

And this is, in a sense, a *regression to the origin of
the culture of humanity prior to the creation of language.*
However, remember that
this is **spiral development** as well.
It is obviously a regression to the origin that has
climbed up one step higher.
An *advanced culture of non-linguistic communication*
has been born, in which
modern sophisticated media technology is used.

If so, as a result, what will happen?

A paradigm shift will occur
from ability for *thinking* and *logic*
to ability for *feeling* and *intuition*.

*From the **culture of thinking***
*to the **culture of feeling**—*
such a paradigm shift will occur.

And as a result of this paradigm shift,
not only the ability
*to think about something **logically***
*by reading **texts** and **words**,*
but also the ability
*to feel something **intuitively***
*by viewing **photos** and **videos***
will be refined.

However, we must not misunderstand this.
This never means that our **ability for language**
or **ability for logical thinking** will diminish.

What will happen moving forward is definitely
a **dialectic development**.

*Different abilities which appear to be **in opposition***
*will become **integrated** and **sublated**.*

For example,

Ability for thinking *versus* ***ability for feeling***.
Ability for logic *versus* ***ability for intuition***.
Reason *versus* ***sensibility***—
such pairs of *abilities considered previously as opposites*
will become integrated in us as one single ability.

If we think back, in the industrial society or
knowledge society up until now,
it has been emphasized
in school and corporate education
to develop our own abilities of
thinking, **logic** and **reason**.

However, in the *post-knowledge society* going forward,
it will become more important to develop the *abilities of*
feeling*, *intuition *and* ***sensibility*** rather than
the abilities mentioned above.
In this sense, in the *trend of **image communication***
created by the **Web 2.0 revolution**,
we will realize an ideal balance in terms of
developing our abilities as humans.

In recent years, these words have been often discussed:

Right brain *versus* ***left brain***.

These words need to be considered carefully
from the viewpoint of dialectic **sublation**.

A *da Vinci society* will arise, where anyone can develop various talents in the manner of Leonardo da Vinci.

Now, *what will happen in our lives going forward?*

Various shifts will occur:
from monetary economy to voluntary economy,
from beneficiary innovation to participatory innovation,
from indirect democracy to direct democracy,
from linguistic communication
to non-linguistic communication,
from a culture of thinking to a culture of feeling.

When such paradigm shifts occur,
just what kinds of changes will happen
in each of our lives?

From **single talent**
to **multiple talent**—
this paradigm shift will occur.

That is, *instead of leading a life which develops*
only a single talent,
we will be able to lead a life which can develop
various talents.

This is because, through the various kinds of
paradigm shifts discussed earlier,
we can, for example, lead such lives.

In the daytime, we work as managers in a company,
on the weekends, we work as members of NPOs or NGOs.
And, when we have time, as individual consumers,
we belong to Web communities which carry out
prosumer-based development by joining in the development
of new products and interacting with the companies.
Moreover, in our own social media, we deliver
various messages and enjoy comments from many people.
In addition, we make public our own photos on websites,
and occasionally we perform our own songs
and release them in our own social media.

We will be able to lead such lives.
If so, what kind of society will arise going forward?
We could venture to say.

A *da Vinci society* is it.

Leonardo da Vinci was a multitalented genius
and an outstanding figure in the Italian Renaissance.

A da Vinci society is one
in which *we can develop the various talents
sleeping inside us, express ourselves freely,
and make public our works to society
in various fields including hobbies and learning,
science and technology, art and music, prose and poetry*,
even if each of us is not a genius like da Vinci.
Moreover, everyone will be able to participate in
the creation of the culture of their society.
Such a society will arise in the near future.

The *post-persona society* will arrive, where anyone can live various *personalities*.

Now then, in such a **da Vinci society**,
what will happen next?

*From a **single personality**
to a **multiple personality**—*
this paradigm shift will occur.

This is because, in essence, for humans,
***talent** and **personality** are two sides of the same coin.*

In other words,
developing the **talent**
needed for one profession or job is,
at the same time,
developing the **personality**
needed for that profession or job.

For example, through working as a manager,
a **leadership personality** is developed in that person.
Through working as a scientist or engineer,
a **logical personality** is developed in that person.
Through working as an artist or musician,
a **sensory personality** is developed in that person.

Therefore, in the **da Vinci society**,
we will *cultivate various **talents***, and at the same time
we will *also cultivate various **personalities***
sleeping inside us.

And actually,
these will bring about a great paradigm shift in our lives.

Because, in society up to now,
in many cases, we were living a single personality.
In order to make our life and work go smoothly,
we would often choose the most suitable ***persona***,
and by wearing it, we would try to avoid
conflict with others and confusion in our lives.

However, as a result, what has happened?

Suppression has happened.

We have noticed *the existence of many **personalities***
within our self through various experiences in our lives.
But since living these personalities very often actually
causes misunderstandings and confusion
in real daily work and life,
we have been living while ***suppressing*** *most of them*
and avoiding their exposure.

To discover, accept and express

the *hidden self*

is none other than *catharsis*.

However, that situation changed
through the **Web 2.0/3.0 revolutions**.

Because, through these revolutions,
we have *become able to live various **personalities***
without creating confusion in our daily work and life,
and without producing misunderstandings
from those around us.

In the daytime,
we live a personality as a manager in a company,
and on the weekends,
we live a personality as a social entrepreneur.
In the world of the Web, we lead our life as a designer
participating in product development,
and on our own social media, we lead our life
as a novelist or essayist.
And at times we lead our life as a photographer
holding an exhibition on websites
or as a musician performing our own songs on websites.

In this way,
we can *live and express*
*the various **personalities***
*which we suppressed behind our **persona*** up until now.
Such a ***post-persona society*** will arrive.

If so, why does this have an important meaning?

322

*Because it is **catharsis**.*

*To discover the **suppressed self** or the **hidden self**,*
accept it, and express it—
this is a profound **catharsis** for a person.

Despite this, in society up to now,
most people have been required to
live a **single personality**.

It was, in a sense, needed to maintain social order,
while it caused unconscious **suppression**
deep in the minds of people.
At times, it caused *individual mental illness*,
and at other times, it caused
social-psychological illness.

Of course, we should not forget that
the **Web 2.0 revolution** and **Web 3.0 revolution** will not
solve all the problems of individual illness and social illness
and that *social-psychological illnesses unique to*
the world of the Web can arise.
But these revolutions have made us notice
that there exists a complex system inside of our minds.

It is an ***ecosystem of mind***.

That is, *various personalities exist in our minds*
*and they form a single **ecosystem**.*

If so, what does this mean?

Management of the *ecosystem of mind*
will allow the abilities of
humans to flower.

The coexistence of *diverse values*—
this is the meaning.

That is, *our activities to discover, accept and express
the diverse personalities within ourselves
mean that we accept the coexistence of
diverse values within ourselves.*

And this has one important meaning.

That is because,
when we recognize the **diverse personalities**
and accept the coexistence of
diverse values within ourselves,
a wonderful thing will happen.

The flowering of abilities—
this is what will happen.

For example, *abilities of imagination and creativity,
insight and intuition, sensibility and empathy,
expression and communication*—
these abilities will flower within us.

For example,
let us consider outstanding creators in art and literature,
excellent leaders in management and politics and
superior innovators in science and engineering.
All of them create wonderful works through
embracing **multiple selves** inside of them, and
through contradiction and conflict,
dialogue and collaboration, among their multiple selves.

However,
to recognize the **diverse personalities** inside oneself and
to accept the coexistence of **diverse values**
is an easier process said than done.
At times, this is precisely
the *very painful experience of a psychological process* of
conflict between opposing values and struggle with contradictions,
which most of the outstanding people above have experienced.

And for that very reason, this psychological process,
in many cases, will be tied to
growth and maturation as a person.

Consequently, in the coming age, the following matters
will become *important concerns in our lives:*
how to discover, accept, and express
*the various **personalities** in ourselves,*
*how to manage the **ecosystem of mind** that*
consists of those various personalities.

And these actually
will become very important concerns
not only for individuals
but also for society as a whole.

Why is this?

The coexistence of *diverse values* in the individual mind will realize the coexistence of *diverse values* in society as a whole.

This is because *the **coexistence of diverse values** will be required of the whole society as well.*

Especially today, in advanced states that
proclaim democracy,
many people believe that
*cultivating a lot of diverse values and accepting them
in their society
is a proof of the **maturity** of their society.*

This stems from a deep reflection on the fact that
in the history of the 20th century,
states that were tainted with a single ideology
oppressed people who did not accept it,
invaded other states that did not agree with it,
and caused calamitous wars.

However, if we watch
the realities of the world in the 21st century,
even in *democratic states that
advocate the importance of **diverse values**,*
bipolarization and division of public opinions
have been advancing in a serious way, and
anti-immigrant ideas have been spread and empowered.

In addition, with the end of the Cold War,
the old ideological opposition between ***capitalism*** *and*
communism appeared to come to an end,
but as we have seen in the world since 9.11,
a new ideological opposition has intensified between
Christianity *and* ***Islam***,
and the **new Cold War** has begun between
autocratic states such as Russia and China and
democratic states such as Western countries,
holding the risk of nuclear war.

If so, why have
deviations towards a single set of values
ironically occurred in societies
where the ***coexistence of diverse values*** is advocated?

The reason is actually obvious.

That is because, *in the minds of each of us,*
such a ***coexistence of diverse values***
has not yet been realized.

In *society as a whole*, no matter how much it is said
that the coexistence of **diverse values** is important,
if *each individual* cannot accept **diverse values**
in their mind, secret prejudices and contempt
as well as enmity and conflict will continue
in obscure corners of society.
And when a single value system acquires power,
an autocratic tendency will often arise to make
that value system penetrate into society as a whole.

For this reason, in the coming age,
the *management of the* ***ecosystem of mind***
in individuals will become extremely important.

A paradigm shift will occur

from *ideology*

to *cosmology*.

Now then, in the coming age,
what kind of *paradigm shift should occur
in society*?

*From **ideology**
to **cosmology**—*
this paradigm shift should occur.

That is, what humanity learned from
the various experiences of the 20th century is that
*the current paradigm exposed its limitations.
In this paradigm the people proud and steadfast
in their single-minded **ideologies**
clashed and fought with each other
and attempted to
assimilate the world into a single **ideology**.*

If so, what kind of paradigm should spread
throughout the world in the 21st century
in place of this **ideology** paradigm?

It is the ***cosmology** paradigm.*

This is a paradigm in which we do not reject
any of the various value systems existing in the world,
but accept them tolerantly.

It is a paradigm in which
we learn the respective positive points of
various value systems and incorporate them,
and appreciate the new values that will emerge from
the encounters of the various value systems.

In recent years, the importance of *pluralism*
that accepts the diversity of value systems
has been mentioned by many intellects.
But, often, the words *coexistence of diverse values*
has been misunderstood and used in the sense of
**tolerating different values and
accepting their coexistence**.

However, the *true meaning* of these words is
*recognizing the coexistence of different values
as the greatest value*
and this is none other than the **cosmology** paradigm.

In Chapter One
I stated that
the essence of evolution is diversification.

Now, in the same sense,
the *evolution of the society* in which we live means
the diversification of the value systems in our societies.
And by this diversification,
the evolution of society will be promoted,
the future possibilities for evolution will expand,
and a **truly wealthy society** will be realized.

Now then, when this paradigm shift
from **ideology** to **cosmology** occurs,
what kind of paradigm shift will occur
in the *world of religion*?

Monotheistic religious systems

will regress to their origin,

to *polytheistic* religious systems.

From **monotheism**
to **polytheism**—
this paradigm shift will occur.

Why will this occur?

Because the laws of dialectic also apply,
without exception, to the development of religion as well.

The law of **spiral development**—
this will happen.

In other words,
old religions will be revived in new forms.

It is **polytheism**.

To discuss polytheism,
we need to ask one basic question.
What kind of religion was the earliest one
if we look back in the history of humanity?

It was ***animism***,
according to which gods and spirits
resided in everything in the world.

And what appeared after **animism**
was ***polytheism*** in which various gods existed
as symbolized in Greek and Roman mythology.

But that **polytheism**, in the course of world history,
relinquished its primary status to
monotheisms such as
Judaism, Christianity, and Islam.

A major reason for this was that the *doctrine of*
monotheism was established
on the basis of a clear single value system,
and came to have a *consistent refined system*
for leading many people into the world of faith.

However, in all things,
a strong point is always a weak point as well.

Monotheistic religion,
since it is a system with a clear value system
and a consistent doctrine,
always created the ***exclusionist tendency***,
which means that
it could not coexist with other **monotheistic** religions.

This became the reason
for the disputes between religions
and wars between religious states
that have been repeated throughout world history.

Religious systems

will evolve into a *religious system at a metalevel*, based on the principle of *cosmology*.

Now, what will happen to this **monotheism**?

A **spiral development** will occur.

*From **polytheism** to **monotheism**,
and again,
from **monotheism** to **polytheism**—*
such a regression to the origin will occur.

Remember again,
this is also dialectic development,
spiral development.

A revival of **polytheism** in a new dimension,
and a *dialectic sublation of **monotheism** and **polytheism***—
this is what will happen.

If so,
what form will it take?

*The various **monotheisms** existing in the world*
will not negate other doctrines,
will accept the existences of other doctrines,
will understand the basic commonalities of
various doctrines
and will coexist in the world.

In this way, *a world of **polytheism** in a new dimension*
will emerge in human society.

Aldus Huxley once showed,
through various examples in his ***The Perennial Philosophy***,
that *many religions* which had emerged in human history
speak common truths
in the foundations of their doctrines.

The **polytheism** that will be revived in the future
will become a ***religious system at a metalevel***,
which understands the common truths
in various **monotheistic** doctrines,
and does not negate any doctrine,
but rather accepts every doctrine.

And this new religious system will
go beyond the two opposites of
monotheism and **polytheism**
and become an ***evolved religious system***
by sublating these two dialectically.

In a sense, this will become the trend
to occur at the same time as
the paradigm shift from **ideology** to **cosmology**
mentioned earlier.

The *Gaia philosophy*, a major concern of this period of global environmental problems, is a revival of ancient *animism* in a new form.

However, when considering the evolution of
religious systems in the 21st century,
we need to understand one more interesting trend.

It is the *spiral development of **animism**.*

As mentioned earlier,
animism,
according to which gods and spirits reside in everything,
was regarded as **faith of uncivilized people** or
primitive religion and faded away
with the appearance of **polytheism** and
the evolution of religious systems into **monotheism**.

But this **animism**
was **revived** in an unexpected place
late in the 20th century.

That is *the world of **science**.*

It was revived in the scientific world
in the setting of major issues that humanity faces now:
The global environmental problems.

If so, in what form was it revived?

It was in *the **Gaia** philosophy.*

That is, the scientific theory stating that
the Earth itself is a gigantic living system
was advocated by the British scientist, **James Lovelock**,
and has gained the support of many scientists.

Lovelock has accumulated research results for many years,
and proposed that the system called Earth
is a gigantic **living system** that has *homeostasis*.

In other words, it is the *idea that life resides in
everything in this world, this Earth*.
This is, in a sense, spiral development of
the nostalgic **animism** and a **revival** of it
in a more sophisticated form.

And when we examine the revival of **animism**
and the regression to **polytheism**,
we will notice an interesting fact.

The fact is expressed in a worldview that has been stated in
Buddhist Thought for thousands of years.

The words
*"in mountains, rivers, grass, trees, lands: everywhere
resides the Buddha nature, no matter where."*—
this is the idea that **the Buddha nature** resides in
everything on the Earth, as does **life** itself.
This is, in a sense,
sophisticated animism.

And this Buddhist Thought is also a religious system that
already has involved *Mahayana thought* in its basis,
which is the *cosmological* principle
that incorporates all doctrines and ideas within itself.

A paradigm shift will occur in the scientific world from the *mechanical system worldview* to the *living system worldview*.

In this way,
when *religion* undergoes a paradigm shift,
what kind of paradigm shift will *science* itself undergo?

This has already been discussed since the 1960s.

*From the **mechanical system worldview**
to the **living system worldview**—*
this paradigm shift will occur.

That is, it is a paradigm shift
*from the worldview regarding this world
as a **gigantic machine**
to the worldview regarding the world
as a **great living system**.*

The reason this paradigm shift
has come to be needed in science is
that *reductionism*, which has been the basis of science
up until now, faces its limits.

Reductionism is based on the belief that
we could understand the nature of the world
if we deconstruct this world, like a machine, into
small components, analyze each component carefully
and finally synthesize the results.

But this research method has faced its limits.

In other words,
this world is like an organic living system,
and by the procedure of deconstructing and analyzing it,
its original nature is lost.
As a result, it becomes impossible
to understand its nature.
This problem was pointed out as the *limit of*
reductionism.

This is a problem which is symbolized by the fact that
we cannot understand the causes of psychosomatic illnesses
through only detailed physical examination, nor can
we understand group psychological phenomena
through only the psychoanalysis of individuals.

Consequently, the limit of this **reductionism**
was proclaimed from as early as the 1960s
as a basic criticism of **science**.
Also it was proclaimed in different forms
as a criticism of the *Newtonian paradigm*
based on Newtonian mechanics, and of
the *Descartes paradigm*
presupposing the separation of mind and body.

On the other hand, though ***holism***, which was proposed
as a criticism of such **reductionism**,
was agreeable as one idea,
it lacked any *specific methodology* to implement it.

However, in the 1980s, a specific methodology,
interestingly enough, was born from
the very modern science that holism was criticizing.

The *science of complex systems* will bring about the evolution of modern science into the *science of the living system paradigm.*

What is that method?

It is *the* **science of complex systems**.

This is a leading edge science and
an extremely broad interdisciplinary research field
begun at the **Santa Fe Institute**
established in New Mexico, USA, in 1984
by the three Nobel Prize winners
Murray Gell-man, **Philip Anderson** and **Kenneth Arrow**.

So, what are *complex systems*?

There are words which teach us its meaning:

When things become complex,
they acquire new properties.

Just as the words suggest,
including all of nature, society, and humans,
when such systems become complex,
they acquire **new properties**,
which are not the **simple sum** of
the properties of their constituent components.

And, to research these new properties that
complex systems acquire is one of the objectives of
the science of complex systems.

If so, what are these **new properties**?

The cultural anthropologist, **Gregory Bateson**,
gave a profound insight:

In complex things, life dwells.

As these words suggest, when all systems,
including nature, society, and humans, become complex,
they begin to manifest *as **living systems** with properties
of self-organization, emergence, coherence, evolution,
co-evolution, and the formation of ecosystems.*

And, to elucidate this phenomenon is
the **ultimate objective** of complex systems science.

Now what will happen through the emergence and
development of complex systems science?

This is the paradigm shift in **worldview**,
discussed earlier.

It is the paradigm shift
from the **mechanical system worldview**
to the **living system worldview**.

However,
this paradigm shift to the **living system worldview** has,
in fact, occurred
not only at the leading edge of **science**
but also at the leading edge of **technology**.

The Internet revolution has brought about the evolution of organizations, markets and societies into *sophisticated complex systems.*

What is the leading edge of **technology**?

It is the *Internet revolution*.

Now then,
why will this revolution promote a paradigm shift
to the **living system worldview**?

It is because *the Internet will transform all
social systems into living systems*.

That is, because the Internet will enhance
the *interrelationships* among the internal constituents
in the systems of organizations, markets and societies,
enhance the *complexity* of these systems,
and promote their properties as *complex systems*.
Consequently, the Internet will promote the properties of
self-organization, emergence, coherence, evolution,
co-evolution and the formation of ecosystems
in those systems.

Actually, in the Internet world,
the following phenomena has occurred everywhere:

Self-organization of online communities.
Emergence of new knowledge in communities.
Coherent behavior of many people through the Internet.
Co-evolution of the culture of the company and
the consciousness of the consumer.
Formation of product ecosystems at online shops.

Now then, as a result, what has happened?

*The permeation of the **living system worldview** into*
the consciousness of people—
this is what has happened.

In other words, as people engage in activities
in the Internet world,
the consciousness of people will naturally transform
into the **living system worldview**.

If so, what will be needed as a result?

The wisdom to cope with the living system—
this is what will be needed.

For example, in living systems such as organizations,
markets and societies,
wisdom to promote self-organization of communities,
wisdom to promote emergence of new knowledge,
wisdom to generate coherence among people,
wisdom to promote the formation of ecosystems—
such wisdom will come to be needed.

The *wisdom to cope with the living system* will be needed to solve global environmental problems.

However, in the coming age,
in addition to the Internet revolution,
there is another important reason that
the *wisdom to cope with the living system* will be needed.

It is *global environmental problems*, including
global warming.

These problems will also require us to learn
the **wisdom to cope with the living system**.

There are two reasons for this.

*The first reason is that the Earth itself is
the **largest living system**.*

That is,
as described by James Lovelock's **Gaia philosophy**,
the Earth itself is
a *gigantic living system* with homeostasis and is
the *most sophisticated complex system* that
nature has created over 4.6 billion years.

Therefore, if we want to engage in
solving global environmental problems,
first of all we will need to learn the *wisdom
to cope with this **gigantic living system***.

342

The second reason is that
the global environmental problems themselves form
*an **extremely sophisticated complex system**.*

That is, global environmental problems are
highly complex issues, involving a very large number of
elements including the Earth, nature, society, culture,
economies, politics, institutions, organizations,
science and technology.
To solve them, we need the wisdom to cope with
highly complex systems, that is,
the *wisdom to cope with a **sophisticated living system**.*

Taking ***change in human lifestyle***
as just one example often stated as a solution to
global environmental problems,
what is necessary to make such change in lifestyle will
not be pressure by government from above, but will be
movement created from among the people themselves
in spontaneous, self-organizing and emergent ways.

But, for this, we will need to adopt
*a **policy of emergence** or a **strategy of emergence***
combining various types of approaches as follows:

Development and provision of inexpensive and easy-to-use
environmental technologies,
introduction of economic incentive systems
to promote change in lifestyle,
formation of communities
where people influence each other, and
utilization of media
to change the environmental culture of society.

This is also the **wisdom to cope with the living system**.

The *wisdom for living system* that resides in the *ancient civilizations* of humanity will revive.

Now then, where is this kind of **wisdom**?

To put it concretely, typical examples are
the wisdom to cope with
organizations, markets, and societies
evolving towards a **living system** and
the wisdom to cope with the global environment
as a **gigantic living system**.

From where should we learn about
*the **wisdom to cope with the living system** and*
*the **wisdom for living system***?

The answer lies in a mysterious paradox.

*The wisdom that resides in **ancient civilizations**—*
this is what we should learn from.

This is because, in every country in the world,
ancient civilizations always embraced
*the **living system worldview** in their foundations.*

For example, as mentioned earlier,
it is said in the ancient Buddhist Thought in Japan that
"in mountains, rivers, grass, trees, lands: everywhere
resides the Buddha nature, no matter where."

There is also the word *Jinen* in Japanese Buddhist Thought.

344

This word also expresses a deep philosophy related to
self-organization and emergence.

Another example is a thought described by
the Native Americans:
The earth, we are borrowing it from our descendants.
This is also a thought for living system
that transcends time and space.

Similarly, let us consider
the religions and myths, legends and tales,
fables and fairy tales existing everywhere on earth.
They always describe the world we live in
as a world that is a living system,
and tell us the wisdom for living in that world
through the heroes and heroines of those myths and tales.

In this way, in the ancient civilizations of every country,
the **wisdom for living systems** richly abounds.

However, *we often consider*
ancient civilizations** as **backward civilizations.
But that perception is incorrect.

Once the cultural anthropologist, **Lévi-Strauss**,
showed the keen insight into the *pitfalls of*
using the words **civilized** *and* **primitive**.
He related that he found
outstanding wisdom in various forms
among those people we call **primitive**.
Just as he expressed, in **ancient civilizations**
sleep a lot of superior **wisdom for living systems**.

Now, if that is so,
what will happen going forward?

The wisdom of *ancient civilization* will merge with the science and technology of *modern civilization* and will create a *new civilization*.

The spiral development of **civilization**—
this will happen.

In the near future,
the **thought and wisdom for living systems**
which had resided in **ancient civilizations**
will be revived in a new form.
And this will merge with
science and technology,
organizations and institutions
which have been fostered in **modern civilization**.

And this will be extremely important when
thinking about social changes and innovations
which humanity will need to deal with
in the 21st century.

This is because science and technology, and
organizations and institutions
will be limited due to the **thought** and **wisdom** that
exist in their backgrounds.

For example, in the present age,
when we are faced with various problems,
we tend to lay the *blame* on
science and *technology*, as well as *capitalism*.
But, **science and technology** and **capitalism** themselves
are not the roots of these problems.

346

Operationalism by which we want to handle the world
according to the desire of our ego,
and the *mechanical system worldview*,
a projection of **operationalism**,
by which we want the world to behave
like a machine that can be freely manipulated—
both of these factors existing in the background of
science and technology and **capitalism**
are precisely the roots of the problems.

That is, if **science and technology** and **capitalism**
are combined with **deep thought and wisdom**,
it would become a force greater than before
to generate coherence and empathy among many people,
to enhance their consciousness, to change the culture of society,
and to change society from its very foundation
by spreading widely throughout all of society.

In particular, *when modern science and technology
combine with ancient wisdom for living systems,*
a *new civilization* will be created right there.

For example, let us take the Japanese idea of *Mottainai*,
which has globally spread through the advocacy of
the Nobel Peace Prize winner Wangari Maathai.
This idea considers resources as precious and
wants to avoid throwing them away by reusing them
according to ancient wisdom.
When this good ancient idea is connected with
modern leading edge recycling technology,
the new *resource recycling civilization* of
the 21st century will be born.

Also, a *natural energy civilization* and a mature
symbiotic civilization of the new age will emerge.

When ancient *wisdom for living systems* and modern *science and technology* merge together, a great force for social change will be created.

And this **new civilization** will not be one in which **thought and wisdom for living systems** is applied only in the field of **environment**.

It will be a civilization in which **thought and wisdom for living systems** is applied in various fields such as *education*, *communication*, *community* and *medical care*.

For example, let us take the mind sensitive to the mysteries residing in nature and to the wonders of nature, and the thought of putting a high value on the *sense of wonder* as advocated by Rachel Carson.
When this thought is connected with educational systems using leading edge technology including ultra-high resolution, 3D imaging and virtual reality, a new paradigm of *experience-based nature education* will be born.

Also, there is the thought of putting a high value on people's mutual communication of **tacit knowledge** inexpressible in words through images and without using language.
When this thought of non-verbal communication is connected with a sharing system of photos, computer graphics, images and videos in the world of the Web, a new paradigm of *image communication* will be created.

Furthermore, let us consider the Japanese *thought of*
enishi (a destined relationship),
which interprets meetings in life between people as
encounters that were **destined to happen**
and had some deep meaning.
When this thought is connected with
the culture of the online community,
a new paradigm of an ***encounter community***
will be born.

There is also the idea of ***mitori*** (terminal care),
in which the dignity of persons passing away is respected
and family members watch over their last moments.
When this thought is connected with
the leading edge medical care systems,
a paradigm of ***mind care hospice*** with deep humanity
will be created.

In this way,
when *the **deep thought and wisdom for living systems***
*residing in the **ancient civilization** and*
*the **leading edge science, technology**,*
organizations and institutions
*fostered in **modern civilization***
connect and merge together,
we will see the birth of a ***new social system*** and
the birth of a ***new paradigm civilization*** right there.

However, if in each country, a spiral development between
ancient civilization and **modern civilization** occurs
in this way,
in fact, it can be foreseen that a spiral development
will occur on an even more magnificent scale.

What kind of spiral development will this be?

Spiral development will occur between

Eastern civilization and

Western civilization.

It is *the spiral development of*
Eastern civilizations *and* ***Western civilization***s.

That is what will happen.

Why is this?

Because, if in a country, a spiral development occurs
between **ancient civilization** and **modern civilization**,
then, the same kind of spiral development
will occur in humanity as a whole.

If so, what is the ***ancient civilization***
in humanity as a whole?

It is ***Eastern civilizations***.

If we look back on the history of humanity,
the dawn of civilization began with
four Eastern civilizations:
Egyptian, Mesopotamian, Indus and the Yellow River.
And these civilizations were extremely
primitive civilizations from the viewpoint of
modern highly developed civilizations.
But in their foundations lay deep **religious grounds** and
fertile **conceptions of living systems**.

However, the center of the civilizations of humanity
shifted from there to the west.
Western civilization first flowered in
Greece and Rome, and then, with its center in Europe,
developed superior science and technology,
fostered sophisticated art and culture,
and created capitalism.

And, entering the 20th century, the center of that
civilization moved further to the west.
That is because, in a country called America,
which was founded in the New World
by immigrants from Europe,
science and technology flowered even further
and capitalism achieved rapid development.

That is, ***modern civilization*** *in humanity*
as a whole is now ***Western civilization***
centered in the West.

Consequently, what will happen going forward
on a historical scale is the *spiral development*
and the interpenetration of
Eastern civilization *and* ***Western civilization***.

The **thought and wisdom for living systems** residing in
Eastern civilization will be revived and will merge with
the leading edge **science and technology** and **capitalism**
fostered in **Western civilization**.

Such a spiral development will occur.

If so, in what way
will the merging of these two civilizations occur?

The merging of Eastern civilization with *science and technology* and *capitalism* has already begun.

Actually, this merging has already begun.

For example, let us consider **Silicon Valley** in the US.
This is an advanced region
which should be called the leading edge of
science and technology and **capitalism** in the world.

When we enter a bookstore in this region,
we will notice something odd.

The shelves are laden with
books on science and technology
such as computer science and biotechnology,
books on business administration
such as venture business and management.

But oddly enough,
there are also other kinds of books piled up beside them:

Zen Buddhism, *Taoism*, *esoteric Buddhism*, and
Indian philosophy.

Such books on **Eastern Thought** are always there.

What does this mean?

Also, in Europe,
the merging of both civilizations has begun.

352

For example,
let us take the *Gaia philosophy* mentioned earlier.
This new paradigm, the view of the Earth
which has influenced environmental protection movements
around the world, actually is a very Eastern view of
the Earth as a living system as well.

And in the midst of the deepening of
global environmental problems,
the German economist **Ernst Schumacher**
is gaining appreciation once again.
The *thought of small is beautiful*, which he advocated,
is also an Eastern Thought.
The **Buddhist economics**, he advocated, symbolizes this.

Now then, what is happening in Japan,
one of the Eastern countries?

In this country as well, for a long time,
the *merging of Western capitalism and Eastern Thought*
has been attempted.

This is so-called
Japanese style capitalism and management
which is based on *Eastern views of*
work, compensation, organization, and talent.

For example, ***working*** in Japanese *means*
for neighbors' happiness.
So, Japanese style capitalism is based on
such views of work.

And then, these trends to connect Eastern Thought with
science and technology and **capitalism**, in fact,
have begun to occur in various forms all over the world.

The age of
the *prehistory* of humanity
will come to an end.

Now, in the history of humanity,
when Eastern civilization and Western civilization thus
achieve spiral development
and merge together,
what will happen in the future?

I dare to say,

*The age of **prehistory** will come to an end.*

That is, for the history of humanity,
the age of its **prologue** will end.

This is because when Eastern civilization and
Western civilization merge together,
the most harmonized civilization
for humanity will be born.

Science and technology and **capitalism**
that have been developed by Western wisdom.
Thought and wisdom for living systems
that have been deeply rooted in Eastern grounds.

When these two merge together,
a **new civilization** will come into the world.

And when opening the door to that **new civilization**,
we will *obtain an important key*
to solving various problems for all humans
from global environmental problems
to population explosion, food crisis, resource exhaustion,
energy crisis, as well as starvation, poverty,
discrimination, conflict, terrorism and war.

And some day,
when we have solved these problems
through the **new civilization**,
the **prehistory** for humanity will end.

From then,
the **true history** for humanity will begin.

The science fiction master, Arthur C. Clarke,
who passed away in 2008,
wrote a novel titled ***Childhood's End***.

As in that title,
*we humans will end our **childhood**, some day*.

It will be the moment of truth
when we humans make another great step towards
a new higher level on the spiral staircase of history.

12 Paradigm Shifts That Will Happen

The *voluntary economy* will increase its influence
on society relative to the *monetary economy*.
And a new economic principle will emerge.

Many consumers and citizens
will come to participate in the process of
changes and innovations in society.

Direct democracy will be realized
not only in the field of *politics*,
but also in the fields of *economy* and *culture*.

The mainstream of communication will shift
from linguistic communication
to image communication.

The culture that emphasizes *thinking*
and the culture that values *feeling*
will merge.

The *da Vinci society* will arise,
where anyone can develop various talents
sleeping inside oneself.

----

in the Future of Human Society

The *post persona society* will arrive,
where anyone can express *multiple personalities*
hidden beneath one's persona.

The value system in society will shift
from *ideology* which emphasizes a single value
to *cosmology* which accepts diverse values.

The age of exclusive *monotheism* will end,
and the age of *new polytheism* will begin,
where various religions will coexist.

The basis of science will shift
from the *mechanical system worldview*
to the *living system worldview*.

The merging will occur between
the *science and technology* of modern civilization and
the *wisdom for living systems* of ancient civilization.

Eastern civilization and Western civilization
will learn from each other, and
a *new civilization* in the 21st century will be born.

Part III

The *Five Crises* Facing Humanity

The Pitfall of the *Progressive View of History*

Now, having finished Part I and Part II,
what are your feelings and thoughts
on the future of humanity?

In this book, I have spoken only of a ***hopeful future***
with regard to the future of humanity.

However, with the various crises facing humanity presently,
not a few readers may feel
less **hope** and more ***anxiety* about the future**.

With that in mind, here at the end of this book,
I would like to take a broad view of the crises facing humanity
and discuss how we should go about dealing with them
from the perspective of the ***dialectic view of history***.

However, in order to do so,
I must first warn you of a *pitfall* we are likely to fall into
when foreseeing the future.

That pitfall is the ***progressive view of history***.

To put it concisely, this is the view that
*history proceeds in the direction of **human progress***.

For example, the following points represent some of the ways
in which this view of history is expressed.

1. The world may pass through periods in which
   there are systems of slavery, aristocracy, tyranny, etc.,
   but it will always be moving towards a democracy in general.

2. The world may have wealth gaps,
   but it becomes wealthier overall,
   and the wealth gaps eventually shrink.

3. The world has experienced a variety of wars and conflicts,
   but it will eventually establish world order
   and achieve lasting peace.

4. The world, as globalization progresses through
   the movement of people, goods, money and information,
   will eventually become one great economic sphere.

5. Human science and technology will continue to develop,
   and that development will bring prosperity and happiness
   to humanity overall.

History Which Develops *Dialectically*

This *progressive view of history*,
which many historians and thinkers
have spoken of and believed in over the years,
tells us of the *macroscopic direction* in which
history progresses with a sense of *hope*.
However, this way of thinking
tends to create a fantasy in our minds that
the world moves linearly in a positive direction.

One example of this is
the book *The End of History and the Last Man*,
published by American political scientist and economist
Francis Fukuyama in 1992.

This book was written to express hope for
the future of humanity at the end of the cold war
as the Soviet Union and
other Eastern European autocracies collapsed.
In it, Fukuyama writes of the victory of democracy
as the ultimate form of human society, and
of a lasting economic prosperity for society.

Unfortunately, however,
the reality of history since then is not so simple.
As I explained in Part II,
dialectical developments occur, such as
the development through *spiral process,*
development through *negation of negation,*
development through *transformation*
from quantity to quality,
development through *interpenetration of opposing objects*,
and
development through *sublation of contradiction*.

These cause *twists and turns*
which at times can lead to developments
which seem like *regression and backstepping* rather than
progress and advancement.
We must not forget that this is the way history develops.

Five Realities of the Modern World

Actually, looking at the realities of the modern world,
anyone would hold the following doubts about
the *linearly progressive view of history* mentioned above.

1. It was believed that
   the whole world would move towards democracy
   due to the collapse of Eastern European autocracies
   starting with the Soviet Union;
   in reality, however, *states under autocracies*
   are increasing more than those under democracies.

2. It was believed that
   the whole world would become more prosperous
   due to the development of capitalism, and that
   wealth gaps would shrink;
   in reality, however, *wealth gaps in the world overall have*
   become wider than ever in the history of humanity, and

economic gaps within each country are further widening.

3. It was believed that, with the end of the cold war,
there would be no more large-scale wars; in reality,
however, conflicts and wars are increasing
in regions all over the world,
and now that Russia has finally invaded Ukraine,
humanity once again faces the threat of nuclear war.

4. Due to the COVID-19 pandemic,
the world experienced global restrictions on
the movement of people and goods, and
due to the Ukraine crisis,
struggles for energy and food have intensified,
causing the world to move not towards
an interdependent global economy (or a world economy),
but rather *towards searching for*
an independent single-state economy
which does not depend on other countries.

5. It was believed that
the development of science and technology
would bring blessings to humanity as a whole and
enhance people's sense of happiness;
in reality, however,
scientific and technological advancements
and material prosperity alone do not give us
a sense of happiness, and many people are
therefore *beginning to return to religious ethics.*

Now then, what exactly is going on here?
Let us consider
what is happening from a **dialectic** point of view.

A Great Return of *History's Pendulum*

Development through **negation of negation** is occurring.

That is, a **reversal** is happening.

The pendulum which was moving towards **democracy**
is now returning to **autocracy**.
The pendulum which was moving towards **economic equality**
is now returning to **economic disparity**.
The pendulum which was moving towards **world peace**
is now returning to **war and crisis**.
The pendulum which was moving towards **world economy**
is now returning to **single-state economy**.
The pendulum which was moving towards
science and technology is now returning to **religious ethics**.

By putting it in this way,
there are surely readers who have some doubts.

So, humanity is not *progressing*, but rather *regressing*.
So, the *future* of the world will *become worse* than the past.

It is natural to think this.
Looking at the *surface phenomena* of what is happening
would naturally lead to such conclusions.

However, we must look at a *deeper level of phenomena*.
Remember what I explained in Part II and you will see why.
I explained there that **dialectic**,
as the law by which the world develops,
is the *process of development*
through **thesis, antithesis, and synthesis**.

364

The *True Meaning* of Development through *Thesis*, *Antithesis*, and *Synthesis*

This process of development
through **thesis**, **antithesis**, and **synthesis**,
which is the *fundamental dialectic law*,
is the process by which
an ***antithesis*** is born *in opposition to a **thesis***, and
both undergo dialectic ***sublation** (aufhaben)*,
leading to a final ***synthesis*** on a higher plane.

However, this does not simply mean,
in a sense of **linear logic**, that
the ***thesis*** *and **antithesis** fight one another, and that
the superior one is the winner.*

The true meaning of this is that
thesis *and **antithesis** both **learn from one another***, that
the two ***incorporate each other's exceptional aspects***, and
this represents none other than
a **dialectic** *interpenetration*, or ***sublation***.

To put it another way,
true development cannot occur without the process of
maturation, or humbly ***learning*** and ***incorporating***
the **opposing side's exceptional aspects**.

In the world today, it seems that
many trends are reversing themselves—
the trend towards **democracy** is reversing
in the direction of **autocracy**,
the trend towards **economic equality** is reversing
in the direction of **economic disparity**,
the trend towards **world peace** is reversing
in the direction of **war and crisis**,
the trend towards **world economy** is reversing
in the direction of **single-state economy**, and
the trend towards **science and technology** is reversing

in the direction of **religious ethics**.

The reason for this is that
*democracy and **capitalism**, **pacifism** and **globalism**,
and also **science and technology**,
are not yet fully **matured** and*
the *dialectic process* of **learning** and **incorporating**
has not fully *progressed*.

The Pride of Post-Cold War *Democracy*

For example, in the world today,
the reason **democracy** has not taken root and
autocracy is spreading is that
*modern **democracy** still has many problems.*

*Decision-making takes time and work,
policies often lose persistence,
populism easily spreads*—
as long as **democracy** carries problems such as these,
it will be easy for the pendulum
to swing back towards **autocracy**.
The cause of **autocracy**'s revival can actually be found
in modern *democracy's fragility*.

That is, **democracy** must,
in its opposition to **autocracy**, mature into
*a democracy that can make decisions quickly,
a democracy that can maintain persistent policies*, and
a democracy that aims for the true benefit of its people.
If **democracy** cannot thus mature,
autocracy will easily be revived again and again.

The misfortune of **democracy** is that, due to
the repeated collapse around 1990 of **autocratic states**,
with the Soviet Union at its core,
a *prideful thought that*

366

democracy has gained a historic victory was born, and
this **pride** caused us to neglect the task of
further reforming **democracy** and
making it an even more excellent political system.

Because of this,
democracy as the true form of progress for humanity,
still has many reforms it must undergo
in order to be realized universally across the globe.

These reforms include
reform of voting systems,
spread of digital democracy, and
introduction of AI-driven government functions.

Specifically, I believe that
the **introduction of AI-driven government functions** is
an important key to reforming and maturing **democracy**, but
let us save that discussion for another opportunity.

The Overconfidence and Arrogance of Post-Soviet *Capitalism*

In the same way, if modern **capitalism** is
failing to bring prosperity to humanity as a whole,
widening the gap between the poor and wealthy,
the reason for this is that
capitalism has not yet become a *system* which
appropriately distributes wealth nor
a system which is sustainable.

As mentioned above,
the Soviet Union and other Eastern European states
collapsed around 1990,
causing us to think that
the *historic experiment of socialism* had ended in failure.

Another misfortune for humanity is that
capitalism fell into a certain *overconfidence and arrogance*
at that time.

As a result, modern **capitalism** failed to humbly accept
the *criticism and problems suggested by socialism*
to reform itself into a *mature capitalism*
that incorporated the good aspects of **socialism**,
but *over bloated a warped capitalism*
that may be called **gluttonous capitalism**.
And what this over bloating brought about was
environmental destruction, overuse of resources,
widening of the wealth gap, and
rampant spread of selfish values.

However, because the various societal problems
brought about by this **gluttonous capitalism**
have been steadily escalating,
in recent years phrases like
stakeholder capitalism and *sustainable capitalism*
have cropped up and a future vision of capitalism
that is mature, evolved, and deepened,
has been discussed and sought after all over the world.

I also wrote about this *future vision of capitalism*
in *Invisible Capitalism*,
which I published in 2009 around the time
I served as a member of the Global Agenda Council of
the World Economic Forum (Davos Forum).

The Reason *Regression* and *Backstepping* Occur in History

Now, as I have explained already,
the world progresses and develops through
the *dialectic process of thesis, antithesis, and synthesis*.
However,
as is clear from the example of **democracy** and **autocracy**,

as well as that of **capitalism** and **socialism**,
when **thesis** is overconfident of its superiority to **antithesis**,
and fails to actively address its own problems,
when **thesis** does not see **antithesis**
as a mirror from which to humbly learn,
we fall into *overconfidence and arrogance*
which prevents **dialectic development** from occurring,
and we do not progress to
a *world in which **thesis** and **antithesis** merge and*
*sublate each other's exceptional aspects in **synthesis***.

In such a case,
the pendulum swings from **thesis** back to **antithesis**,
resulting in a situation which seems like
mere ***regression*** and ***backstepping*** is occurring.

The Fragility of *Globalization*

It follows, therefore, that the world's swing
from ***world economy*** to ***single-state economy***
is occurring for the same reason.

Looking back on recent decades,
with the rallying cries of ***globalization***,
we have been convinced that
becoming a single global economy would be an ***absolute good***,
and we have raced to achieve globalization
while turning our eyes away from the concern that
***an interdependent system** is*
***easily linked to crisis** and*
reveals its fragility in times of war.

However, through
the worldwide COVID-19 crisis and the Ukraine conflict,
we are finally beginning to realize the dangers of
a **global economy** and an **interdependent system**.
Furthermore, the world has closed its eyes to

the extremely *fundamental problem* that is
the flipside of flashy words like
globalization and **economic growth**:
how will all the people in the world live
with the limited resources found on Earth?
But that same world will face a harsh reality in the near future.

That is, the *scramble for globally limited resources*
such as energy, food, water, and minerals,
which has certainly intensified between various countries,
will lead to fierce conflict with the Ukraine crisis as a trigger.

This means that, in each country, not only will
the *shift from* **world economy** *to* **single-state economy**
be accelerated, but
we will also be forced to confront the problem of
how all the people in the world can live
with the limited resources found on Earth.

The Essential Cause of *War*

Now, we must gain a deep understanding of
the fact that this fragility of globalization is
the *essential cause* of the shift of humanity's circumstances
from **world peace** *to* **war and crisis**.

That is, with the Russian invasion of Ukraine,
we have been preoccupied with
the opposition of Russia against NATO and the US,
and the threat of nuclear war.
But for humanity,
a more *essential and serious cause of war* is
the *fierce battle for Earth's resources* which
each state will escalate going forward.

To put it another way,
if we are to talk about true **world peace**,
we must move beyond the level of UN Security Councils,
military forces, and peacekeeping operations
to find a solution to the worldwide *fierce battle for resources*
such as energy, food, water, and minerals.

The Words That Will Lead Humanity to Ruin

Now, in order to find such a solution,
we must have the *wisdom to face directly the cold reality* of
where humanity will be led, ultimately, by the words that
each state's government now uses as a matter of course,
and which we have accepted as a matter of course:
economic growth, and **competitive strategy**.

In other words,
if all states continue to maintain *economic growth*,
thinking **we must continue to grow no matter how far**,
the cold reality is that
all of Earth's resources will eventually be completely used up.
If all states continue to maintain *competitive strategies*,
thinking **we must not lose to other states**,
the cold reality is that
the scramble for Earth's limited resources will escalate and
what was originally **economic competition** will eventually
develop into **military expansion competition** and **war**.

We must have
the *courage and wisdom to directly face this* **cold reality**.

The Success of *Science and Technology*, and its Overconfidence

Now, why is it that a return
from **science and technology** to **religious ethics** is occurring?

371

The cause of this can also be found in
the overconfidence of **science and technology**.

It is apparent that
there are truly remarkable achievements in the development of
science and technology up until modern times, and that
this development has brought about
wonderful **material prosperity** and
convenience of livelihood.
However, that very success also led to
the overconfidence of **science and technology**,
which came to believe
it could promote **a sense of happiness** in people
without the help of **religious ethics**.
For this reason, **science and technology** has focused on
the pursuit of **material prosperity** and **material satisfaction**,
but it has neglected
the pursuit of **spiritual prosperity** and **spiritual satisfaction**.

If so, what has occurred as a result of this?

Confident though **science and technology** have been,
material prosperity and **convenience of livelihood**
have not brought people a **true sense of happiness**.

Though *material prosperity* brings initial **brief happiness**,
it also gradually stimulates a desire in our hearts
to **become even more prosperous**, and
this desire grows without limit,
causing us to fall into
a *chronic **sense of lack** and **sense of incompletion***.

Convenience of livelihood also brings initial **brief happiness**,
but our subconscious gradually becomes dominated by
ideas of **efficiency** and **speed**
which form in the background of **convenience**,
causing us to fall into
a *chronic **sense of frustration** and **sense of obsession***.

372

In other words,
even when *science and technology* develop this far,
if it is only enhancing
people's **material prosperity** and **material satisfaction**,
and failing to enhance
our **spiritual prosperity** and **spiritual satisfaction**,
then it is inevitable that
many people will not feel **true happiness**,
and this will lead them to return to **religious ethics**.

Despite this, **science**, based in materialism,
has not humbly learned from **religion**, based in spiritualism,
and has failed to reassess its very basis and
broaden its horizons by stepping into the realm of
people's **spiritual prosperity** and **spiritual satisfaction**.

That is the fundamental reason that a return is occurring
back to **religious ethics** from **science and technology**.
This is a misfortune for **science and technology**,
but there is also another misfortune here.

Tradition and Adherence of *Religious Ethics*

That misfortune is the fact that
religion, too, has fallen into *overconfidence*.

In other words, **religion** has adhered to the thought that
*this religion's teachings, which have been transmitted
throughout history, are the eternal truth, and that
people will be saved if only we continue to
protect and believe in these teachings.*
Because of this adherence,
religion has neglected to allow
the light of a new age to illuminate those teachings
so that it may evolve and deepen into a new form.
Specifically, despite the long series of
leading modern scientific discoveries,

such as **quantum entanglement**, **dark energy**,
and **parallel universe theory**,
which can only be described as **mystical**,
modern religions refuse to consider deeply and
learn the meaning of such discoveries,
fail to shed the light of cutting-edge knowledge
onto their ancient teachings, and continue to believe that
they can save people through their traditional teachings.

The *overconfidence of these two*, **science** and **religion**,
is the reason that people who return to **religious ethics**
due to being spiritually unfulfilled by
science and technology and **material prosperity**,
still fail to attain spiritual satisfaction.
Science and **religion** must both realize this **overconfidence**
and, through self-reform, move towards further maturation.

The Fundamental Problem of *Human Consciousness*

Now, as I have stated previously,
in the world today, it seems that
many trends are reversing themselves—
the trend towards **democracy** is reversing
in the direction of **autocracy**,
the trend towards **economic equality** is reversing
in the direction of **economic disparity**,
the trend towards **world peace** is reversing
in the direction of **war and crisis**,
the trend towards **world economy** is reversing
in the direction of **single-state economy**, and
the trend towards **science and technology** is reversing
in the direction of **religious ethics**.

The reason for this is that
democracy and *capitalism*, *pacifism* and *globalism*,
and also **science and technology**,
are not yet fully **matured**.

374

Now, actually, the fundamental cause of this is clear.
It is because the very **human consciousness**,
which is the foundation for all of these notions,
is not yet matured.

No, I, the author, do not mean to speak as a critic
from an elevated perspective.
What I mean to say is that,
it is because the **consciousness of us people, individually**,
including myself, is not yet matured.

Democracy and Populism

For example, the reason for *democracy* being swayed
towards **populism** and **lobbyist politics**
clearly has something to do with the politicians
who advocate for such systems, but,
fundamentally, this happens because we are swept up in
self-interest which leads us to choose politicians who
will benefit us personally,
though they may cause a loss in benefits
to society as a whole and to future generations.

To give another example,
the reason **democracy** loses to
dictatorship and **authoritarianism** may be partly
because of the clever *demagoguery and propaganda* of
dictators like Hitler,
but as social philosopher **Erich Fromm** sharply pointed out
during World War II in his book ***Escape from Freedom***,
there was a mob mentality or social psychology
which caused the people of that time to attempt to escape
from the **responsibility that came with freedom**
by relying on a strong leader.

Capitalism and the Vulture Fund

Also, let us consider **capitalism** being transformed into
what could be called *avaricious capitalism*,
a form of capitalism which pursues **profit**
through any means necessary.
A representative example of this is the *vulture fund*,
a financial organization
which ensures **high returns on investments**
even if it ignores its effects on society and the public, and
which has run rampant in our markets.

However, the *avarice* of the **vulture fund** is not
something which was born suddenly and without reason.
We must realize that,
actually, it was the countless *small desires* of each of us,
mindlessly searching for
financial packages with just a slightly better yield,
which gave birth to such *avarice*.

Of course,
in opposition to this **blindness** of countless investors,
there is an enlightened movement of
socially responsible investment (SRI)
which is spreading through society.
However, we must not forget that
the transformation of **capitalism** into **avaricious capitalism**
is caused by our individual **consciousness**.

Internationalism and a Sense of Discrimination

Furthermore, the reason
principle of international cooperation loses to
antiforeign nationalism is surely not because of
the appearance of a powerful *antiforeigner leader*.
Rather, it is because there is a desire
in the hearts of many citizens for *antiforeigner policies*, and

376

the appearance of such an **antiforeigner leader** is rather
a ***mirror*** *reflecting the consciousness of the citizens.*

That is, if there is even the **faintest trace** of
racial discrimination, ethnic supremacy,
or antiforeigner nationalism in the consciousness of us citizens,
then ***international cooperation*** will easily lose to
antiforeigner nationalism when national circumstances
become difficult.

This was illustrated
during the Eastern European refugee crisis of 2015,
when then-German Prime Minister Angela Merkel
sincerely pleaded with her country's people, saying that
*"I want Germany to be a country that
extends a helping hand to suffering people"*—
The fact that she went on to lose her next election
perfectly symbolizes
what I am saying about antiforeign sentiment.

The Fragility of *Pacifism* and Consciousness

Now, the above **refugee problem** is not the only circumstance
in which the racial discrimination, ethnic supremacy, and
antiforeigner nationalism
sleeping within our hearts will surface.
On the contrary, this is only a ***prelude***.

As I have already stated,
countries across the globe will soon begin a fierce battle
for resources such as energy, food, water, and minerals.

And it is extremely likely that
this will cause conflict and war between each country.
At that time, I'm afraid we will experience great suffering
while we learn of the ***fragility*** of the ***pacifism***
touted after the war.

And this **fragility** will not be the *fragility of systems*
such as the UN Security Council and UN peacekeeping forces,
or even peace treaties and security treaties, but rather
the *fragility of consciousness* which causes
the racial discrimination, ethnic supremacy,
and antiforeigner nationalism
in each of our hearts to surface with ease
the moment we are faced with confusion and crisis.

How to Cope with the *Self-interest* in Our Hearts

As I have explained above,
the fundamental reason that
democracy and *capitalism, pacifism* and *internationalism*,
have not sufficiently **matured** yet, is that
our individual consciousness has not yet matured.

Specifically,
our consciousness is easily swayed towards *self-interest*
when faced with confusion and crisis.

Actually,
when we are faced with various confusions and crises,
we are often swayed by the thought that
I just need to protect my own country's interests,
I just need to protect my community
and company's interests,
I just need to protect my own interests.

Because of this, if we truly want humanity
to overcome the various crises now facing it,
we must find the *wisdom to cope with the* **self-interest**
in each of our hearts.

However, when we talk about this **self-interest**,
we immediately hear the voice of those
who advocate **religious ethics** which says,

378

we must not be swayed by self-interest and
we must attain a heart of altruism.

Of course, no one will deny that this is the right thing,
but the unfortunate reality we see when looking back upon
thousands of years of **religious** history, is that
wars were not ended, wealth gaps were not closed, and
discrimination was not eliminated by these words.

Rather, in actual society,
while **altruism** is preached to people,
the **activity of self-interest** of people only expands, and
words of altruism are, at times,
mere *mimicry* and *hypocrisy* to hide **selfish activity**.

The Road to Dialectic Sublation of *Self-interest* and *Altruism*

Now, the ideas of
self-interest and **altruism**
have opposed and fought one another
over the several thousand years of human history—
are they impossible to reconcile?

No, I don't believe that is true.
These two will also
undergo **dialectic** *merging and sublation.*

The result of this will be the idea of *rational altruism*
I explained in Part I, Chapter Four.

That is,
seeing **self-interest** and **altruism** not as opposing ideas,
but rather considering that
treasuring other people is in one's own best interest,
treasuring the benefit of society is
in one's own best interest, and

treasuring the benefit of future generations is
in the best interest of the current generation.

We must work to spread
this very *idea and movement of* **rational altruism**
throughout the world.

If so, how can we go about spreading this idea and movement
throughout the world?

When *Science* and *Religion* Join Hands

One important method is that
I mentioned in Part I, Chapter Four.
That is, *for* **science** *and* **religion** *to join forces.*

In other words,
the *righteousness* of **rational altruism** could be shown
through *scientific proof*, while
the *idea and movement* of **rational altruism** could be spread
through *religious passion.*

For example,
let us take the report titled **"The Limits to Growth,"**
published in 1972 by the global think tank **Club of Rome**.
Through various scientific simulations,
this report showed clearly that
humanity must make its living
while sharing the limited energy, food, and resources
available on our small planet.
And even today, *cutting-edge science* has unravelled
the mechanism of *global warming*
and clearly shown that
the world as a whole will be ravaged by climate crises
if we continue on as we have up until now.
These scientific activities changed people's consciousness and
led to greater *environmental protection movements*,

380

which various religious organizations even participated in.
However, **science** must not stop at global environmental crises,
but rather use the *combined power* of *natural science*,
social science, and *human science* to address
crises of democracy and capitalism,
as well as internationalism and pacifism, showing us
the *righteousness and importance of **rational altruism***, and
joining forces with **religion** to
spread this idea and movement throughout the world.

The *Prehistory* of Humanity Will End

Now, in the face of humanity's various crises,
there is talk of various reforms, such as
the *reform of the **democratic system*** or
the *reform of the **capitalist system***.
Of course, we should be decisively advancing such reforms,
but, as I stated in this Part III,
without our individual ***reform of consciousness***,
no ***reform of systems*** will have the power
to overcome such crises.

Looking back, humanity has walked
a historical path for thousands of years
hoping for this ***metamorphosis of human consciousness***,
but has been unable to achieve it.

However, now, as we face a *grave crisis of human existence*,
we must make an utterly new attempt at achieving
this **reform and metamorphosis of consciousness**.

This ***utterly new attempt*** will be overcoming
the opposition of ***science*** and ***religion*** to merge them together,
which we have failed to achieve
over the past several hundred years.

When that happens,
the *altruism* continuously preached by *religion*
up until now, and
the *rationalism* continuously touted by *science* up until now,
will undergo dialectic sublation, and
rational altruism will spread throughout the world.

This alone is the *road to the survival of human civilization*
in the 21st century, and a road to further development.

And when we embark on this road to further development,
when **science** and **religion** join forces
and human civilization overcomes various crises,
the curtain will finally rise.

*Humanity's **prehistory** will end, and*
*the curtain will rise on the age of **true history**.*

This book was written in hopes that
such a curtain indeed will rise.

Acknowledgments

First of all, I would like to express gratitude for
my acquaintance with Dr. Jacques Attali,
which became the catalyst for the creation of this book.
It was through a dialogue with him at an international event
that we had our first encounter.
However, it was the e-mail I received from him
after he had read my English book
that marked the beginning of everything.

> I read with great interest "The Five Laws to Foresee the Future"
> and I found a great convergence with my work. I would be
> honored to engage in a deep conversation with you about the
> future.

Once again, I am grateful for this destined encounter.

Furthermore, the Part II of this book,
"The 'Five Laws' to Foresee the Future," is
a revised version of the book by the same title
published by Kobunsha in 2008.
I would like to express my gratitude to
Mr. Toshikatsu Furutani, former Executive Director
at Kobunsha, for his efforts in publishing this book.

I would also like to express my gratitude to
Mr. Takahisa Miyake, Director at Kobunsha,
for his editing of Part I,
"The *Twelve Insights* to Foresee the Future,"
and his efforts in publishing this book in its entirety.
As always, conversations with Mr. Miyake
shed new light on my work.

Furthermore, I would like to express my gratitude to
Mr. Tomoki Hotta and Mr. Hisao Nishimiya from Babel,
as well as translator Mr. Christopher Zambrano,

for their assistance in translating
the content of my lectures to Dr. Jacques Attali.
The translation work put in by this team was perfectly in sync,
and I am very grateful for it.
I also dedicate this book to the late translator Ms. Rieko Sasaki,
who passed away last year.
I believe she is celebrating the publication from afar.

I would like to express my gratitude to
Ms. Kumi Fujisawa, Chairperson of
the Institute for International Socio-Economic Studies.
Conversations with Ms. Fujisawa regarding
what will happen in the future
always fostered the **emergence of wisdom**.

I am also grateful to my family, who constantly support me
in various ways: Sumiko, Sayer, and Yue.
In January of this year, a severe cold wave hit the world,
but somehow, this area near Mount Fuji had little snowfall, and
I wondered at how much smaller the snow-cap
upon the peak of Mount Fuji was compared to previous years.
When I gaze at Mount Fuji shining against the blue sky,
the lyrics of that song come to mind:
On a Clear Day, You Can See Forever.

Lastly, I dedicate this book to my late parents.
In this life steeped in contradictions,
I seek profound meaning within those contradictions.
I have learned the importance of living in such a way
from both of you.

February 17, 2023
Hiroshi Tasaka

Profile of the Author

1951   Born.

1974   Graduated from the University of Tokyo Faculty of Engineering.

1981   Earned a Doctorate in Nuclear Engineering from the University of Tokyo Graduate School of Engineering. Joined a private company in the same year.

1987   Became visiting researcher at the U.S. think tank the Battelle Memorial Institute.

1987   Became visiting researcher at the Pacific Northwest National Laboratories (the U.S.).

1990   Joined in the establishment of the Japan Research Institute.
Promoted visions and strategies for the creation of new industries driven by the private sector. Over a decade, established and managed 20 consortia with 702 companies from various industries.
Held various positions, including a board member and the Head of the Center for Strategy of Emergence.
Currently a fellow at the Japan Research Institute.

2000   Professor at the Tama University Graduate School. Lectured on social entrepreneurship and social business. Currently a Professor Emeritus of the Graduate School.

2000   Founded and became the president of Think Tank SophiaBank, aiming at creating the paradigm shift of social systems in the 21st century.

2003   Established and became the representative of the Japan Social Entrepreneur Forum (JSEF).

2005   Selected as a US-Japan Innovator by the Japan Society in the U.S.

2008   Appointed to the Global Agenda Council of the World Economic Forum, host of the annual Davos meeting.

2009   Began attending the TED Conference annually as a TEDster.

2010	Appointed as the Japanese representative of the Club of Budapest, an international association of intellectuals including 4 Nobel Peace Prize laureates serving as honorary members.
2011	Appointed as the Special Advisor to the Prime Minister of Japan following the Great East Japan Earthquake and the Fukushima Nuclear Power Plant Accident. Worked on nuclear disaster response, nuclear administration reform, and energy policy change.
2013	Established Tasaka Juku, a forum of 8,500+ executives and leaders worldwide that aims to foster "New Paradigm Leaders in 21st Century" by integrating 7 intelligences: "thought," "vision," "mission," "strategy," "tactics," "skills," and "humanity."
2023	Appointed as the Chairman and the Chancellor of the Akademeia 21st Century, world's largest academy for Cool Japan.

Professor Tasaka has published over 100 books, including books in English *"Hiroshi Tasaka Talks about the Future of Humanity"*, *"Five Laws to Foresee the Future"*, *"Invisible Capitalism"*, *"The Wisdom Forgotten"*, *"The Staircase Where We Can See the Future"* and *"To the Summit - Why Should You Embrace an Ideal in Your Heart?"*

Currently, Professor Tasaka is actively engaged in publishing and lecturing internationally.

Made in the USA
Columbia, SC
27 June 2024

b47b0bc2-86b2-4c91-a2ed-f8f38ea7b30bR01